W9-BVW-444

FREDERICK DOUGLASS

Marianne Ruuth

MELROSE SQUARE PUBLISHING COMPANY
LOS ANGELES, CALIFORNIA

To the memory of Inger Stevens.

Consulting Editors for Melrose Square
Raymond Friday Locke
James Neyland

Originally published by Melrose Square, Los Angeles.
 Published in the United States by Melrose Square Publishing Company, an imprint of Holloway House Publishing Company, 8060 Melrose Avenue, Los Angeles, California 90046.

Cover Painting: Harry Ahn
Cover Design: Paul M. Papp

FREDERICK DOUGLASS

Melrose Square Black American Series

ELLA FITZGERALD
singer
NAT TURNER
slave revolt leader
PAUL ROBESON
singer and actor
JACKIE ROBINSON
baseball great
LOUIS ARMSTRONG
musician
SCOTT JOPLIN
composer
MATTHEW HENSON
explorer
MALCOLM X
militant black leader
CHESTER HIMES
author
SOJOURNER TRUTH
antislavery activist
BILLIE HOLIDAY
singer
RICHARD WRIGHT
writer
ALTHEA GIBSON
tennis champion
JAMES BALDWIN
author
JESSE OWENS
olympics star
MARCUS GARVEY
black nationalist leader
SIDNEY POITIER
actor
WILMA RUDOLPH
track star
MUHAMMAD ALI
boxing champion
FREDERICK DOUGLASS
patriot & activist
MARTIN LUTHER KING, JR.
civil rights leader
ZORA NEALE HURSTON
author
SARAH VAUGHAN
singer
LANGSTON HUGHES
poet
JAMES BECKWOURTH
mountain man
PAUL LAURENCE DUNBAR
poet
B.B. KING
musician

HARRY BELAFONTE
singer & actor
JOE LOUIS
boxing champion
MAHALIA JACKSON
gospel singer
BOOKER T. WASHINGTON
educator
NAT KING COLE
singer & pianist
GEORGE W. CARVER
scientist & educator
WILLIE MAYS
baseball player
LENA HORNE
singer & actress
DUKE ELLINGTON
jazz musician
BARBARA JORDAN
congresswoman
GORDON PARKS
photographer & director
MADAME C.J. WALKER
entrepreneur
MARY MCLEOD BETHUNE
educator
THURGOOD MARSHALL
supreme court justice
KATHERINE DUNHAM
dancer & choreographer
ELIJAH MUHAMMAD
religious leader
ARTHUR ASHE
tennis champion
A. PHILIP RANDOLPH
union leader
W.E.B. DU BOIS
scholar & activist
DIZZY GILLESPIE
musician & bandleader
COUNT BASIE
musician & bandleader
HENRY AARON
baseball player
MEDGAR EVERS
social activist
RAY CHARLES
singer & musician
CRISPUS ATTUCKS
patriot
BILL COSBY
entertainer
ROBERT CHURCH
entrepreneur

CONTENTS

Chapter One

The Turning Point

ON THE THIRD DAY of September in 1838, a Monday, the weather was fine, a bleak morning sun washing pale light over the streets of the city of Baltimore on the Patapsco River, an arm of Chesapeake Bay. A slight chill in the air announced the approach of winter, and the trees were taking a colorful farewell of summer.

The few people out and about in the early morning hours paid little attention to a young man, over six feet in height, with skin of a golden brown hue, high cheekbones, a broad forehead, and eyes flashing with intelligence,

---

Born into slavery as Frederick Augustus Bailey, Frederick Douglass, after his brave escape to the North, became one of the most prominent speakers in the abolition movement.

as he was walking with firm, decisive steps, determined not to run, though every muscle instinctively pleaded with him to do so. He forced himself to keep walking at a normal, brisk pace, but his heart was pounding madly against his ribs, cold sweat soaking through his red shirt. He also wore a tarpaulin hat and had tied a black cravat carelessly around his neck in sailor fashion. His rich voice murmured a soothing word to a curious dog that had stopped for a moment before trotting off.

He had to steel himself so as not to throw furtive glances over his shoulder, every cell in his body involved in a prayer that he would not be seen by anyone he knew.

His name was Frederick Bailey. He had been a starved boy on the plantation, a houseservant, a field hand, a tradesman at the shipyard. He knew hunger, whippings, unfairness, and humiliation, but he also knew how to read, write, and think. Right now his goal was the Baltimore & Ohio Railroad Station, the first U.S. public railroad, chartered eleven years earlier by a group of local businessmen. He thought of the steam locomotive, black and slowly collecting its power to make its run. He felt at one with that locomotive, because he was also collecting his strength, running for freedom, whatever the

Frederick Douglass fought for civil liberties throughout the world. In 1846 Douglass addressed an English audience during his visit to London, to plead for the Irish Home Rule Act, which would have taken Ireland out of the British Empire.

cost. He knew that the odds were against him, that any person, even a child, could with one word condemn him to a life of hardship without end, destroying his hope forever.

He was a slave. He was a piece of property. Somebody owned him, as they owned cattle and kettles.

Without looking to left or right, he walked, hardly breathing, into the train station but not toward the ticket seller. He had made a thorough study and knew that any dark-skinned individual buying a ticket in the station would have his papers scrutinized (the railroad could be sued if a slave slipped by), while those buying tickets on the train were given less of such inspection. Furthermore, he knew that sailors were treated with peculiar indulgence by train conductors.

The northbound train was due to leave shortly.

He planned to wait close to the wall and jump on the train just as it started, "making a leap in the dark." He thought of the young woman, her eyes large and trusting, who had sold one of her featherbeds to be able to press some money into his hand the night before: Anna Murray, his fiancee. When would he see her again? Would he ever?

The memory of the last time he had tried

to throw off the shackles of slavery and the disastrous result of that attempt lived within him. The appalling defeat returned to torment him, as it had done frequently these last three weeks. The decision to flee had been hard to make. His life in Baltimore lately had been better than ever before in his twenty years on earth; he had warmhearted friends, friends he loved almost as much as he did his life—and then there was Anna. Yet, this was a matter of life and death to him. His choice was to try for freedom or accept slavery forever. He knew he was facing his last chance. If he failed now, he would be given the severest punishment imaginable. Possibly he would die from it. If he happened to survive, he would be put into a position where escape would be impossible.

His body was poised for flight, as at any moment a harsh voice could order him to come along. He tried to melt into the surroundings, become invisible. Had anyone suspected anything? He had taken care to work extra hard at the shipyard near the drawbridge and to take his master all his wages, between eight and nine dollars each week. The previous Saturday his master had been pleased and even given him twenty-five cents, telling him to make good use of the money. He had solemnly promised he would, and had added it to his slim escape fund of seventeen dollars.

The train was arriving, coming to a smooth stop. A few people were boarding. The man stood stock still, furtively studying each person getting on the train. The signal was given for departure. The train began to move. With long steps he ran over to it, climbed up the steps, and went into the car. He sank down on a bench.

Wait, didn't he know that woman? Her glance lingered on him for a moment, then she looked away. He was sure he knew her and equally sure that she knew him. What would she do? She knew he was a slave. And over there the German blacksmith was sitting, a man whom he saw just about every day. Their eyes met. The man might have recognized him, even in sailor's clothing. But he said nothing.

Frederick fingered the paper he carried. It declared that the bearer of the paper—in which a description of an older, shorter, darker man appeared, a description that didn't fit him at all, if anybody had eyes to see with—was a free man, a seaman named Stanley. He was to return this paper by mail to the retired merchant sailor.

The train had traveled for quite a while through Maryland before the conductor came walking through. This was a crucial point. He heard him question another black man harshly and with a great deal of suspicion. But by the time the conductor reached Frederick, who looked up with a confident grin and asked for a ticket, he was in a hurry and scarcely looked at the paper with the American eagle.

At Havre de Grace, the passengers had to board a ferry to cross the Susquehanna River. "Hey, Freddy!" A young black man named Nichols whom he knew and who worked as ferry hand hailed him, throwing several rapid questions at him. What was he doing there? Why in the clothes of a sailor? Stiff with fear that anybody would overhear, he grunted some monosyllabic answers and ducked to another part of the ferry.

On the north side of the river, he boarded the train, which shortly thereafter passed into Delaware, also a slave state. He stayed tense and alert but no longer trying to discover if there were other passengers from Baltimore who might recognize him.

He left the train at Wilmington, the coiled spring of tension remaining within him because the bounty hunters tended to be especially vigilant at border points. Keeping himself in control, he boarded a steamboat headed for Philadelphia. Pennsylvania was technically

An engraving of a view of Baltimore, Maryland, circa 1830. Like many of the southern ports, Baltimore served as a center

of trade, including the slave trade. Many of the ships seen here are carrying slaves to auction—and a life of misery.

a free state, but even there the slave catchers would come looking for runaway slaves. Slave hunting was good business, frequently bringing the catcher one hundred dollars per head.

He had already decided not to stay in Philadelphia but to continue directly to New York, where he assumed he would be relatively safe. Trying to grasp the fact that his feet in the worn shoes were touching free soil, he asked a wizened old black man how to get to New York City and was directed to the Willow Street station. That night he took a train bound for the big city and arrived without a hitch before dawn on Tuesday morning. In less than twenty-four hours, he had ended his slavehood. At least for the time being.

How did he feel? Tired, hungry, practically penniless..., but in writing to his fiancee, Anna, immediately upon his arrival, he said he felt like one who had escaped a den of hungry lions. And yet, feelings of uncertainty and loneliness were soon overtaking him. He could still be caught and taken back to all the tortures of slavery. In the midst of thousands, he was a stranger, with no home and no friends. He dared not reveal who he was and how he had arrived, not to a soul. "I was afraid to speak to anyone for fear of speaking to the wrong one, and thereby falling into the hands of money-loving kidnappers, whose business it was to lie in wait for the panting fugitive, as the ferocious beasts of the forest lie in wait for their prey."

His motto, of necessity, became, "Trust no man!" Every white person was seen by him as the enemy; in almost everyone of color he saw cause for distrust.

He did not dare to go looking for work, and he would soon be out of money. Walking the streets for a few days, he decided to change his name from Frederick Bailey to Frederick Johnson. Finally, in desperation, he turned to another black man, a sailor who seemed like a good sort, and blurted out his story. The man took him to his own house for some food and then contacted David Ruggles of the New York Vigilance Committee, a group that helped runaway slaves to find safe places to live and work. Ruggles took the young man to his boardinghouse at the corner of Church and Lespenard Streets, where they sat down to discuss his future. When told that "Johnson" was a caulker by profession, Ruggles suggested New Bedford as the place where work could be obtained.

Anna Murray, a free black woman, had left Baltimore immediately upon hearing that her Frederick had arrived safely in New York.

Getting slaves out of the South and into the North often required considerable ingenuity. Not all were able to "follow the drinking gourd," traveling overland by way of the underground railroad.

The lithograph above shows Henry Box Brown, who was one of several slaves who escaped by shipping themselves north in boxes, helped by the Philadelphia Vigilance Committee.

Once she was there, Ruggles called in the Reverend J.W.C. Pennington, who, in the presence of Ruggles, a Mrs. Michaels, and two or three others, performed the marriage ceremony on September 15, 1838.

With five dollars as a wedding gift from Ruggles, Mr. and Mrs. Johnson set out on the steamboat *John W. Richmond* for Newport, on their way to New Bedford, Massachusetts, then one of the world's great whaling ports, which meant opportunities for work. The newlyweds spent the night on deck, in conformity with a system that assigned this as the place for "people of color." A stagecoach took them from Newport to New Bedford, but they had no money left to pay for breakfast or to pay the driver, and he took possession of their baggage. What a wedding journey!

Frederick's entire trip from Baltimore to New Bedford occupied less than two weeks.

Ruggles had told him to look up a man named Nathan Johnson in New Bedford. That man and his wife, a kind and well-to-do black couple, took them in. Now came the question of a new name for a new life.

He had gone from "Frederick Bailey" (already as a slave he had dropped his middle names) to being "Stanley" the sailor for the trip and had then in New York decided to call himself "Frederick Johnson," but in New Bedford there were so many Johnsons that he felt the need to change his name a final time. He gave Nathan Johnson the privilege of choosing a name so long as he could keep Frederick in order to preserve some sense of identity. Having just read the long poem *The Lady of the Lake,* by Sir Walter Scott, his quick-witted host at once suggested the name of its hero, Douglass.

Frederick "Douglass" was born, at the age of about twenty (a slave like a horse did not know his or her birthday), in New Bedford, and the name would soon and forever after be synonymous throughout the world with freedom from slavery, with a spirit that cannot be broken, with true heroism, and with eloquence in speech and writing.

WORDS

composed and respectfully dedicated, in token of confident esteem to

FREDERICK DOUGLASS

A Graduate from the

"PECULIAR INSTITUTION"

For his fearless advocacy, signal ability and wonderful success in behalf of

HIS BROTHERS IN BONDS.

(and to the FUGITIVES FROM SLAVERY in the)

FREE STATES & CANADAS.

by their friend

JESSE HUTCHINSON JUN^r.

BOSTON. Published by HENRY PRENTISS 33 Court St.

Chapter Two

The Beginning

A BOY WAS BORN in his grandma's cabin—or in the slave quarters in back of the main house or in an open field—in Tuckahoe, near Hillsborough, Maryland, either in the year 1817 or early in 1818. He was later to say, "I have never met a slave who could tell of his birthday." Not knowing this simple personal fact haunted him all his life, a constant source of frustration. White children knew their birthdays; slaves did not. Sometimes they knew that they were born "during planting time" or "at cherry time." This boy was born when nature was dressed in snow (it could

Among Frederick Douglass's best known written works, "The Fugitive's Song," traces the plight of the slave in America. This was just the beginning of his writing and speaking career.

have been February), as the fourth child of Harriet Bailey, a slave woman in her middle twenties, who named him Frederick Augustus Washington Bailey; the only thing she had to give him was an impressive name.

His father was a white man, but he was never told who he was. For a slave to ask questions about himself was deemed "improper..., impertinent, and evidence of a restless spirit": not good qualities for property to have. (Does the teakettle ask who its maker is?)

The infant was taken from his mother not long after birth, as was common practice: she was sent off to work in the fields, and the baby would be cared for by some woman too old for field labor. It meant that the natural bond between mother and child did not have a chance to develop normally.

He spent his first years in his grandmother Betsey's cabin, on the bank of the Choptank River, in Talbot County, on the eastern shore of Maryland. The cabin's floor and chimney were made of clay, and there were no windows, nor any bedsteads. The boy was an active, happy youngster, although living with a constant fear of being taken from his grandma, as his brother and sisters had been. It happened when he was about six years old, when

Slaves are seen here working the cotton gin on a plantation while their masters stand in the rear counting money. The caption that ran with this engraving stated, "Tell ole Pharaoh to let my people go."

she was ordered to bring him to live at Old Master's house.

About four or five times during his early childhood, his mother made the twelve-mile-long journey on foot, always at night when work was done, to see her son briefly. At sunrise she had to be in the field if she didn't want a whipping. Consequently, he never saw his mother in daylight. He never knew much about her, except that she was the only slave in Tuckahoe who could actually read and write a little, an extremely rare accomplishment.

When he was seven or eight years old, she died, but he was not told about her death until much later. There was no one to ask who had sired him; she took the secret with her to the grave.

"Slavery," he was to observe, "does away with fathers, as it does away with families." He did carry a mental picture of his mother as a tall woman "of deep, glossy complexion and regular features," and when he saw depictions of Egyptian royalty later in life, he stared at them, memories of his mother stirring.

He heard rumors that Old Master himself was his father. Aaron Anthony, called Captain Anthony, a title due to his sailing a craft on the Chesapeake Bay, owned three farms in Tuckahoe and about thirty slaves, for which he had an overseer named Plummer, a drunkard, a profane swearer, and a savage monster, who went around armed with a cowskin whip and a heavy cudgel, two instruments of torture that he used frequently. Once he cut up a woman's head so severely that even Captain Anthony was enraged. That says a lot, since he was himself a cruel man, who seemed to enjoy whipping slaves, male as well as female. Actually, he was a Jekyll-and-Hyde type of character, whose mood would swing from almost paternal affection to the most savage anger. Douglass, whom the master occasionally called "my little Indian boy" (there was something of American Indian in his appearance), remarked of him that he was "a man at war with his own soul, and with all the world around him."

Although a slaveholder himself, Captain Anthony spent most of his time as chief overseer and manager of the estates of the immensely wealthy Colonel Edward Lloyd, known as "the Governor," who owned a thousand slaves and twenty or thirty different farms. Anthony, having all the regular overseers under his control, lived in a brick house near the stately mansion of Colonel Lloyd, representing the greatest luxury imaginable, while outside reigned indescribable suffering.

The boy Frederick saw his mother's sister, his aunt Hester, a beautiful girl in her teens, being whipped brutally several times. The louder she screamed, the harder the master whipped. "And where the blood ran fastest, there he whipped longest," he remembered. He would whip her to make her scream and whip her to make her be quiet. A slave her age had begun to pay court to her, and one night she went out to meet him. The Old Master found out. He brought Hester into the kitchen, stripped her from neck to waist, and told her to cross her hands, which he bound with strong rope. He then made her get up on a stool under a large hook, tied her hands to the hook, and proceeded to whip her, thirty or forty stripes, until her blood was dripping to the floor and she fainted. This was witnessed by Frederick, hiding in a closet, certain that he would be next.

His master's family consisted of two sons, Andrew and Richard, and one daughter, Lucretia, married to a Captain Thomas Auld. They lived also in a house on Colonel Lloyd's plantation, situated about twelve miles north of Easton, on the border of Miles River. Tobacco, corn, and wheat were raised and taken to market in Baltimore by a sloop. Colonel Lloyd kept from three to four hundred

William Lloyd Garrison was a prime mover in the abolition movement. A personal friend of Frederick Douglass, he encouraged his friend to write and speak against slavery.

slaves on the home plantation and more on neighboring farms of his. He was one of Maryland's wealthiest men.

Each month every slave received eight pounds of pork or its equivalent in fish, along with a bushel of cornmeal and a pint of salt. The yearly clothing consisted of two coarse linen shirts, one pair of linen trousers, one jacket, one pair of winter trousers, one pair of stockings, and one pair of shoes. The children who could not work in the field were only given two coarse linen shirts per year. If these didn't last all year, they went naked until the next allowance day, whatever the season and the temperature. Slaves had no beds, only a coarse blanket each, but they were usually so tired during the few hours allotted for sleep that they hardly cared. During his childhood, Frederick had to sleep with his head and shoulders in a sack on cold nights, and his feet had huge cracks in them.

If the slaves did miss, even by minutes, the overseer's summons at sunrise, they were whipped until bloody. One overseer of Frederick's master was aptly named Mr. Severe. When he died, the slaves gave praise to heaven. In his stead came Mr. Hopkins and, although he dealt out whippings, it seemed he took no pleasure in them.

Charles Francis Adams fought in Congress against the Compromise of 1850. Though this bill kept slavery from moving into the frontier states, its effects were weakened by the Fugitive Slave Act, requiring that runaways be returned to the South.

Frederick saw the slaves of his childhood take enjoyment where they could find it, such as in being the ones chosen to go up to Colonel Lloyd's Great House to pick up the clothes and food allowances. Then they would walk through the dense woods, composing and singing songs as they went, loud, long tones, wild notes—coming from the souls of those suffering in bonds, treated worse than cattle. Frederick would later reveal that those who talked about slaves singing as a sign of their contentment, even happiness, did not understand anything. Slaves were singing most and loudest when they were deepest in sorrow and aching most severely.

A finely cultivated garden abounded in fruits of every kind, from apples to cherries, a constant temptation to ever-hungry slaves. The colonel did everything he could think of to keep the slaves out of there, the most successful method being the tarring of the fence. If a slave was caught with any tar upon his person, it constituted sufficient proof that he had tried to get into the garden, and he was severely whipped.

Whipping was the steady and constant punishment for any infraction, real or imagined, large or small.

Since Colonel Lloyd had a thousand slaves,

all told, he did not know them all, nor did those working on farms some distance off know him. One day when out riding he met a man and asked him, in the way of the time, "Well, boy, whom do you belong to?" "To Colonel Lloyd, sir." "Does he treat you well?" "No, sir." "What? Does he work you too hard?" "Yes, sir." "Don't you get enough to eat?" "Yes, sir, he gives me enough, such as it is."

The colonel rode on, and the slave gave no further thought to the man with intense blue eyes and prematurely white hair until a couple of weeks later when men came to chain and handcuff him, after which he was sold to a Georgia trader, never to see his family and friends again. "Sold down to Georgia" was an expression that put fear into the hearts of many, knowing that working the cotton or rice fields in the Deep South was an even harder and quicker way to break backs and spirits.

The slaves learned their lesson, and if any white person asked, they would be full of assurances that their master was kind and fair. Also, having little to be proud of, the slaves took a certain pride in having a rich, powerful master. "It was considered as being bad enough to be a slave; but to be a poor man's slave was deemed a disgrace indeed!" Frederick noted.

Chapter Three

Living with Pain and No Hope

FREDERICK DOUGLASS tells his tales with non-exaggerated intensity, born out of close contact with actual facts, having seen, heard, felt, and breathed slavery from the day he was born until he was well into manhood.

In one of his books about his life, he notes the maxim laid down by slaveholders: "It is better that a dozen slaves suffer under the lash than that the overseer should be convicted, in the presence of the slaves, of having been at fault."

Most of the overseers were cruel beyond belief. Having had a brief spell of an overseer

Most of the slaves that were transported to the Americas came from the west coast of Africa. After being captured by the slave traders, they had to be restrained to prevent them from escaping, either by tying them or locking them within forts.

Many Africans became slaves through tribal warfare. The more powerful tribes preyed on the smaller isolated woodland tribes of West Africa, capturing entire villages to sell them to the

European traders who pulled up to the ports of the Gold Coast to barter for the human merchandise, paying for the slaves with rum manufactured in New England from Caribbean molasses.

such as Mr. Hopkins, who was relatively fair (but he did not last long—not severe enough perhaps?), his place was taken by a Mr. Gore. Severe...Gore...what's in a name?

Gore was a young man but was hardly ever seen to smile and never told a joke. His sharp, shrill voice brought terror to the slaves. He knew how to humiliate further those who were born in deepest humiliation. Once he was whipping a male slave next to the creek. The man jumped into the creek to cool and soothe his stinging, bleeding back. Standing in the water, he refused to come out. "I'll count to three, and if you're not out by then, I'll shoot you." He counted; the slave did not move, and Gore brought up his musket and shot the man. So what happened to Gore? Nothing. He just told both Anthony and Colonel Lloyd that the man was unmanageable and setting a dangerous example to the other slaves.

A man could commit murder and other atrocities and remain a respected citizen of the community! Killing a slave—or any person of color, for that matter—was not treated as a crime, either by the courts or by members of the community. Another master near where Douglass lived killed a slave with a hatchet, boasting of the bloody deed afterwards. A young girl of fifteen was beaten so hard that most bones in her body were broken. It took her a few hours to die in agony. Who did the beating? The wife of a slaveholder, using a stick of oak. What was the offense? The girl was told to mind the new baby in the family. During the night she fell asleep, not having had much sleep for several nights; the baby cried, and the girl did not hear it. That time there was actually an investigation into the matter; the dead girl was dug out of her grave and examined. A warrant was even issued for the arrest of the woman who had done the deed, but the warrant was never served. No punishment, in other words.

Another time, Douglass recalled, an old man, also belonging to Colonel Lloyd, had gone oyster fishing during the night, something slaves would do to get more food into their grumbling stomachs. While fishing in the dark he happened to cross the boundary to the next farm, belonging to a Mr. Bondly. Bondly found him trespassing and shot the man without further ado. The next day he visited Colonel Lloyd, presumably to pay him for his property or give his excuses for what he had done. In either case, it was a trivial matter, and nothing was ever done about it.

Frederick grew up, seeing all this casual

cruelty on a daily basis and yet escaping many beatings due to his charming personality. Since he was too young to work in the fields, his tasks included driving home the cows in the evening, chasing the fowls out of the garden, keeping the front yard clean, and running errands for his master's daughter, Mrs. Lucretia Auld, who took a certain liking to him and used to give him a piece of bread for singing outside her window. During his "free" time, he usually helped the son of Colonel Lloyd, Master Daniel, finding the birds the boy had shot. Daniel liked Frederick and became a sort of protector of the younger boy, whose main sufferings had to do with being hungry and cold, as he went about barefoot and only dressed in the coarse linen shirt of knee-length, whatever the weather. As a slave child, his main food consisted of mush, *i.e.* boiled cornmeal. This was poured into a large wooden trough, which was put on the ground. The children were called, like a bunch of little pigs, and they had to scoop the mush out of the trough. No spoons were given them. They used either their hands or a piece of wood or an oyster shell. The one who ate the fastest got the most; none of the children left the trough feeling satisfied. Until Frederick learned the elbow technique necessary, he used to contend with the dog, Old Nep, for crumbs that fell from the master's table.

Master Daniel would occasionally give him a piece of cake or a candy, and the observant youngster acquired an insight into the contrast between the opulence in the main house and the life of the slaves, whose labor made the luxury possible. There was no schooling for the slave children, except that they were taught, with the help of a whip, to repeat the Lord's Prayer. The rest of their religious training consisted of being told that God up in the sky had made white men to be masters and black people to be slaves, and that He knew what was best for them all.

Chapter Four

A Ray of Light

AT THE AGE OF eight or so, Frederick left Colonel Lloyd's plantation with searing joy in his heart. His master had decided that the boy should go to Baltimore to live with Sophia and Hugh Auld, the brother and sister-in-law of Captain Thomas Auld, who was married to the master's daughter, Lucretia. Being told of this three days before he was due to travel, Frederick spent nearly all his time in the creek, washing himself thoroughly, over and over again. Miss Lucretia had said that people in Baltimore were excessively clean, not like at the plantation. Also, if he could get all

---

The slaves who managed to survive the miserable voyage across the Atlantic were driven from the ships to slave pens in American port cities, from which they would be taken to the auction blocks.

the dirt and the dry skin off, she would give him a pair of trousers. The thought of owning a pair of trousers made his head swim. So he scrubbed and scrubbed himself until his skin was raw.

Since he was a slave, there was little for him to miss when he left. His mother was dead, his grandmother lived far off. He had two sisters and one brother living right there, but their early separation from their mother had nearly blotted out the fact of their relationship from their minds.

To him the move was an exciting change; it was almost a miracle to be the one of all the youngsters on the place to be chosen. Possibly he would encounter hardship, hunger, whipping, nakedness—but such ingredients would be in his life if he were left at the plantation, where he could expect to be only a field hand.

He recalled a proverb of the time: "Being hanged in England is preferable to dying a natural death in Ireland." That summed it up. At least he would be in Baltimore! He had heard about all the wondrous things that city had to offer. However great the Colonel Lloyd house on the plantation, the one with all the pictures on the walls, he was told that it was far inferior to many buildings in Baltimore.

He left with high hopes a Saturday morn-

Slaves here are seen working the cane fields of the South as the overseer watches behind. Many times the slaves were pulled out of the fields to be beaten for the most minor of reasons.

ing, standing on the deck of the sloop as it sailed out of Miles River. In the afternoon of that day, they reached Annapolis and, although he couldn't go ashore, he gaped at the first large town he had ever seen. Early Sunday morning, they landed at Smith's Wharf. On board was a flock of sheep, and the eager boy helped to drive them to the slaughterhouse, after which he was taken to his new home in Alliciana Street in the Fells Point section of Baltimore. On the way, he looked at everything with big eyes, astonished to see that nearly everyone wore shoes!

Mr. and Mrs. Auld were both at home, and he met their little son, Thomas. It would be his job to take care of the cheerful toddler. "This is your Freddy, Tommy." For the first time in his life he saw a white face radiating kindness, that of his new mistress, Sophia Auld. Later he would say that had it not been for this decisive move to Baltimore and especially for Sophia Auld's care when he first arrived, chances are he would have lived out his life as a scarred, overworked, starved plantation slave. What an immense loss it would have been to this nation and its people, black and white.

Sophia Auld lived up to the boy's first impression of her. A gentle, cheerful woman, she had never had a slave under her control. Before she married, she had been making her living as a weaver. At first, young Frederick could not figure out how to behave toward this white woman who did not approve of the servility he had been taught.

Hearing her read the Bible aloud, he asked her to teach him to read. "I was roused from the sweet sleep of childhood to hear the narrative of Job," he said when telling about it later. She began to teach him the alphabet, proceeding quickly to simple words and short sentences, delighted with his rapid progress. Unfortunately, Mr. Auld, a gruff, distant man, who worked as a ship's carpenter, found out what was going on and in no uncertain terms forbade her to continue. He said that it was both unlawful and unsafe to teach a slave to read. "If you give a nigger an inch, he will take an ell. A nigger should know nothing but to obey his master—to do as he is told. Now," he said, looking at the dark-skinned boy, "if you teach that nigger how to read, there would be no keeping him. It would forever unfit him to be a slave. He would at once become unmanageable, and of no value to his master. As to himself, it could do him no good, but a great deal of harm. It would make him discontented and unhappy."

In the earliest days of slavery in the United States, Christianity offered benefits to transported Africans, requiring that any who had lived as Christians before coming to America could not be

enslaved. By the nineteenth century, however, the religion was used by slave owners to justify slavery and to try to make the enslaved accept their lot by emphasizing humility as a virtue.

The words sank deep into the heart of Frederick, actually starting a whole new train of thought. "It was a new and special revelation, explaining dark and mysterious things," he wrote later, even calling it the "first anti-slavery lecture" he had heard.

He knew now wherein lay the white man's power to enslave the black man: in the ignorance of the latter. Consequently he knew the pathway from slavery to freedom: through knowledge, through education. So he continued to learn to read, secretly, without the aid of a teacher, armed with the knowledge that what to Mr. Auld was a great evil was to him, the slave boy, the greatest good, a thing to be sought diligently.

Living in Baltimore, he noticed the difference in the treatment of city slaves. They were better fed and clothed than those on the plantation. No white city man wanted to be publicly known as a cruel slavemaster or at least most of them did not want such a reputation. However, across from the Aulds lived a Mr. Thomas Hamilton and his wife, the owners of two female slaves, Henrietta, about twenty-two years old, and Mary, about fourteen. These two were always starved, always with festering sores and ugly scars from constant whippings and beatings, mostly administered by Mrs. Hamilton, who carried a whip wherever she went. Mary, so starved that she looked years younger than she was, used to fight with the pigs for the offal thrown into the street.

Frederick did go back to the plantation at about nine or ten years of age. His old master, Captain Anthony, had died, and the estate had to be divided among his children. This meant that Frederick had to be present to be counted along with the other property. Men and women, old and young, married and single, twenty-nine individuals in all, were ranked with horses, sheep, and swine. After the evaluation came the division. Of course a slave had no voice whatsoever in any decision as to who would get him or her.

They lined up; men went around taking notes, assessing the flock of slaves to be worth 2,800 dollars. This had to be shared among the three heirs, so the slaves were divided into three lots, each of a value of approximately 935 dollars. "Manhood lost in chattelhood!" Frederick said about this ultimate in human degradation, taking place on October 18, 1827. Trembling with fear that he would fall into the hands of Anthony's son Andrew, a cruel drunkard, Frederick was greatly relieved when he was included in the portion of Lucretia and

Thomas Auld and was sent back to Baltimore to the family of Master Hugh.

Around the same time, Lucretia died, and Frederick found out what had happened to his grandmother, Betsey, who had served her master faithfully. She had peopled his plantation with slaves—she had twelve children and at least twenty-five grandchildren—and had become a great grandmother in his service, rocking the master himself in infancy, working hard during his adult life, and had even closed his eyes when he died. But she remained a slave, now an old slave in the hands of people she did not know. She saw all her children, grandchildren, and great-grandchildren be divided and sold off. Her latest owners, strangers to her, deemed her too old to be of any use, so they left her deep in the woods, in a primitive hut with a small mud chimney, to fend for herself. A very old woman, her body racked with pain, immobility taking over her once so active limbs, she died a slow death, all alone in the wilderness, as everyone was "gone, gone, sold and gone," as the slaves used to sing. Left alone to suffer—and die.

Altogether Frederick Bailey lived in Master Hugh's family about seven years, he succeeded in learning to read and write without any assistance after the very first period. Mistress

When slaves were captured, some traders marked their "property." Sometimes this was done by branding, but other traders cut marks into the skin to create scars.

Sophia had complied with her husband's wishes to the letter. Being a naive, kind soul, she had at first considered it natural to treat the boy just like another human being. Slowly she was instructed to behave differently. "Slavery proved as injurious to her as it did to me," said Frederick Douglass, who saw a warm, compassionate woman change into a hard, angry person. If she saw Frederick even looking at a newspaper, she would snatch it away from him furiously. She kept close watch on him. If he stayed alone too long, she came running to check that he was not looking in a book.

But the boy, by nature endowed with a charming personality, made friends with white boys he met in the street. He converted each one of them into a teacher. When he was sent on errands, he snuck along any piece of reading he could find and by hurrying he found time to stop, talk to boys, and learn a little each time. It helped that he was well fed in the Auld household and able to put bread in his pocket when he went out. This he gave to white boys, many of whom were hungry street urchins. These boys would even talk about slavery with him, expressing lively sympathy with his plight.

He scoured the gutters and retrieved miscellaneous papers, including pages of the Bible, which he cleaned, dried, and studied. At about twelve, he decided he would not be a slave for life. He got hold of a book, *The Columbian Orator*, which contained a dialogue between a master and a slave, in which the master brought out all arguments in behalf of slavery, but the slave had impressive answers to all of these. As a matter of fact, the slave's eloquent self-defense convinced the master to emancipate him and wish him well. Frederick later wrote that, having read the dialogue "when every nerve of my being was in revolt at my own condition as a slave, [it] affected me most powerfully."

He kept reading all he could lay hands on. In the newspapers he learned about abolitionists, at first being mystified by the word, then learning that these were people, many of them *white* people, who believed that slavery was wrong and should be abolished. He read about human rights—and began to see his enslavers as "a band of successful robbers who had left their homes, and gone to Africa, and stolen us from our homes, and in a strange land reduced us to slavery."

Master Hugh had indeed been right in his denouncement of teaching a slave to read!

The logical consequences were to follow,

although at this time there were moments of agony when the boy envied his fellow slaves their ignorance. The more he learned, the more able was he to see, hear, and feel with greater clarity. The pain of knowing what he had been turned into made him think of killing himself a couple of times, but the hope, sharpening into determination, of freedom kept him going.

At the wharf one day, he helped a couple of Irishmen unload stone. When they found out he was a slave, they said it was a pity ("ye mean, for yer whole life!") and advised him to run away to the North, where there were no slaves. He resolved he was going to do exactly that. But first he was going to learn to write. As he was working by now in Mr. Auld's shipyard, he had seen that the carpenters marked each piece of timber with a letter, S, L, A, or F. (for Starboard, Larboard, Aft, and Forward). During the workers' breaks, he taught himself to write these letters in the dirt. Then again the street boys were his teachers; he showed them the four letters he had learned, challenging them. "Can you do better?" And they wrote down letters, which he incorporated into his fund of knowledge. He wrote with pieces of chalk on fences, brick walls, pavement, wherever. From the boys he learned basic arithmetic the same way.

A feud broke out between Frederick's Baltimore master, Hugh, and the latter's brother Thomas, resulting in Thomas taking his property Frederick from Hugh. The youth had to travel to Thomas's farm near the town of St. Michael's. Frederick suffered less from leaving Hugh and Sophia Auld—between brandy on his part and slavery on hers, they had changed greatly from the kind, happy couple he had first encountered—than from leaving the boys of the Baltimore streets, those who had been his teachers at first and lately rather more his pupils.

Color played no part in their relationship. "Prejudice is not the creature of birth, but of education," he had already observed.

Having been rather well-treated for a slave, he was more determined than ever to run away. "Give a man a bad master," he wrote, "and he aspires to a good master; give him good master and he aspires to be his own master."

As he sailed from Baltimore on the sloop *Amanda*, he paid great attention to the direction that the steamboats took to go to Philadelphia. He planned to escape one day and was collecting all possible information in order to do so successfully.

Chapter Five

The Decision

FREDERICK LEFT Baltimore and went to live with Thomas Auld at St. Michael's in March 1833, fifteen years old and having been absent for seven years. Thomas had remarried after Lucretia's death, and Frederick discovered that Master Thomas and his new wife, Rowena, matched each other in cruelty and stinginess. For the first time since age eight, he was experiencing constant hunger pangs. This was the height of cruelty. Most slaveholders fed their slaves coarse food but saw to it that there was enough of whatever it was. The four slaves in the kitchen—Frederick, his

John Brown was perhaps the most outspoken of the abolitionists. He did not believe in passive resistance but preached violent overthrow of the system, ultimately making his stand at Harper's Ferry, Virginia.

sister Eliza, his aunt Priscilla, and a cripple named Henny—were given half a bushel of cornmeal per week and little else. They had to beg and steal from neighbors or wherever and however they could, often while food was spoiling and getting moldy in the smoke-house of the Aulds. To vent their help-less anger and bitterness, Frederick and his sister Eliza became allies, smartly finding ways to frustrate especially Rowena Auld at every turn. Being treated like dumb animals, they became very good at "disre-membering" whatever they had been told. Lucretia's daughter Amanda, about seven years old and frequently mistreated by her stepmother, would cover for them if she could.

In August of that same year, Captain Auld had attended a Methodist meeting and ex-perienced religion. For a moment, his slaves nurtured a faint hope that this would make him more humane. Not so. If anything, he became more cruel and hateful. Morning, noon, and night, he and his wife kneeled in pious prayers. He invited preachers to the house, stuffing them with food while his slaves, standing behind the chairs, never receiving a smile from the churchly men, suf-fered from searing hunger.

A young devout white man named Wilson proposed Sunday school for the slaves in the area to teach them the New Testament and, having heard that Frederick could read, asked him to assist. Frederick embraced the proposal eagerly, and about twenty slaves showed up for the first session. Already at the second meeting, however, a horde of whites, led by Frederick's master, Thomas, and two other Methodist leaders, drove them off with sticks and stones, forbidding them ever to meet again. Frederick, who had shown most enthusiasm, was warned that he could end up with as many bullets in his body as Nat Turner, the slave who had led the bloody insurrection in Virginia in 1831.

Frederick kept listening and observing. The crippled slave woman, Henny, had fallen into the fire as a child and was terribly burned. Her hands were almost useless—all she was good for was carrying heavy burdens. This girl irritated the master no end, and he used to keep her tied up for hours, returning every so often to beat her until her back and shoulders were raw, often quoting the scriptures while swinging the whip.

Frederick, whose eyes flashed defiance, and the hard master did not get along, to say the least. The latter insisted that easy city life

When John Brown and his followers attacked the federal arsenal at Harper's Ferry, Virginia, to begin their slave revolt, federal troops were sent under Col. Robert E. Lee to put down the insurrection. Brown and the others who survived the battle were

tried and sentenced to be hanged. Abolitionists turned Brown into a martyr for their cause, with writers such as Thoreau and Emerson attacking the federal government after Brown was executed on December 2, 1859.

with his brother's family had spoiled the boy and, in order to break him, he rented him out for one year to "Brother Covey," as "Brother Thomas" called him, a poor and supposedly pious man, who rented both his farm and his farmhands. He had a reputation for breaking headstrong slaves and could therefore get healthy young workers for little money.

On the first of January 1834, Frederick became for the first time in his life a field hand under Mr. Covey, to whom it was never too hot nor too cold for outdoor work. It could never rain, blow, snow, or hail too hard. An early, icy-cold morning Frederick was sent out with a team of unbroken oxen to get a load of wood. He had never driven oxen before, and within a short time the animals took fright and bolted, dashing around wildly, upsetting the cart, smashing it with great force against a tree, getting themselves entangled among saplings and underbrush. Finally he managed to straighten them out, load the cart, and start back. At the lane gate, they panicked again, broke the gate, and nearly crushed the young man between the wheel and the post. When boy and team made it back to the farm, he told Mr. Covey what had happened, and this inventive master said he would teach him how to do things. Again Frederick was ordered into the woods, now followed by Covey. There the latter went to a large black-gum tree, cut three big switches, and ordered Frederick to remove his clothes. Since it was bitter cold, the youth did not obey, whereupon the man tore off his clothes and lashed him until the switches were worn out. The sores on his back stayed open for weeks, and the scars remained forever. This was the first of a number of similar whippings.

At Covey's, the slaves were at least given enough to eat but scarcely enough time to eat it. They were in the field from the first hint of dawn and were often kept working until past midnight. Covey was with them, one of the few slaveholders who worked with his own hands, except for the afternoons, when he went home to sleep in order to keep up with the slaves at night. He had a habit of sneaking up on them, even crawling on his hands and knees in the cornfield to avoid detection. Consequently, it was never safe to stop working, even for a minute, and the slaves christened him "the Snake."

Covey had managed to buy one slave, Caroline, a woman about twenty, and told anyone who would hear that he had bought her as a *breeder*. Every night he tied her up with Smith, a married man he had rented for a year. Subsequently she became pregnant and gave birth to twins, quite an addition to his wealth.

This professional breaker of slaves succeeded in breaking Frederick Bailey. "I was broken in body, soul, and spirit," he said later. "I spent this [time] in a sort of beast-like stupor, between sleeping and waking...behold a man transformed into a brute." At times he thought seriously of murdering Covey and then taking his own life, hardly worth being called that. He realized now he was indeed a slave, a slave for life, with no rational ground to hope for freedom.

Covey's unpainted house stood near the shoreline, and Frederick used to watch the beautiful vessels, white sails billowing, on the Chesapeake Bay, seeing them sail off in liberty. The sight tormented him, a constant reminder of his wretched condition. "Oh that I were free!" he would sigh.

The decision to run away one day existed as a constantly beating pulse of hope inside him.

While the first six months at Covey's were pure hell, the second six months grew easier, as things took a strange turn.

In August, on an extremely hot afternoon, the slaves were fanning wheat. Frederick was carrying the mixture of wheat, chaff, and dirt

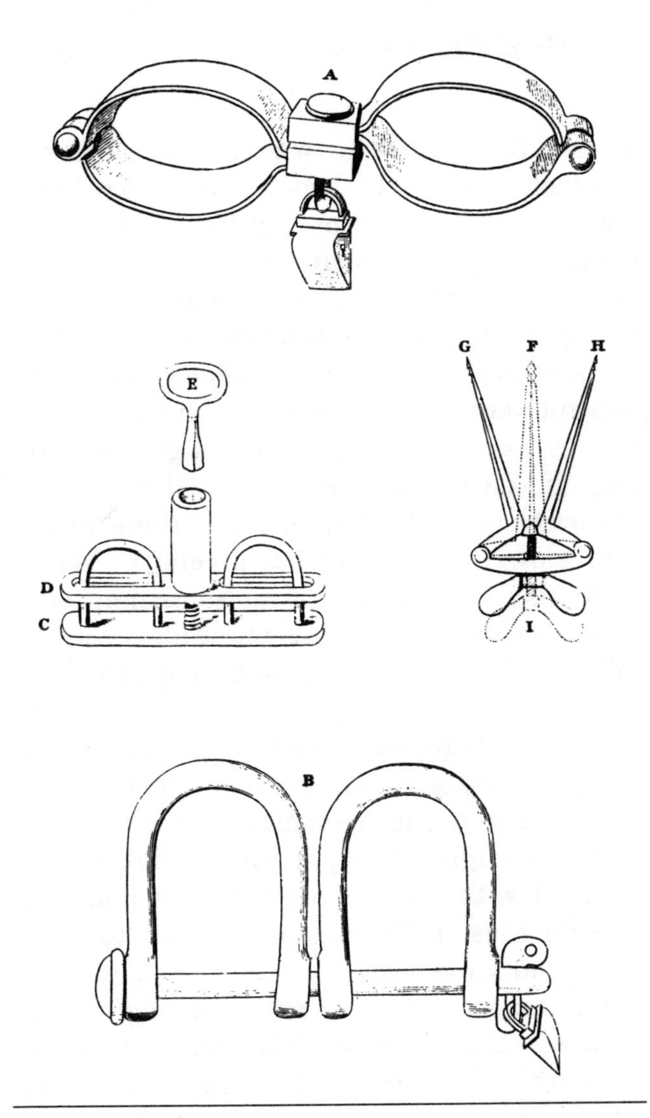

Many means were used to restrain rebellious or strong-willed slaves, including hand cuffs, leg shackles, thumb screws, and what was known as "speculum oris," which forced the mouth of the slave open.

to the fan when he was hit by a fierce headache, began to tremble in every limb, tried to keep on working, but finally fell to the ground, the victim of sunstroke. Mr. Covey up at the house heard the fan stop and rushed to the spot. He kicked Frederick, who still was not able to get up. He then took a hickory slat and hit the young man on the head, making a large wound, from which blood gushed, saying, "If you've got a headache, I'll cure you." Frederick could do nothing but lie there, bleeding, slowly gathering his strength. When Covey became occupied with something else, Frederick decided to crawl off, walk the seven miles to Master Thomas's, and complain about the treatment.

Walking barefoot through bogs and briars, falling down exhausted every so often, he managed to get to his master's, a distance of seven or eight miles, in about five hours. Covered with blood, with torn legs and feet, he told Master Thomas as well as he could what had happened.

His master let him stay the night—but without supper, nor breakfast the next day—after which he had to walk back to Mr. Covey, "that good, religious man, a fine influence on you."

Seeing the worn-out slave returning, Covey

brought out his cowhide whip and a rope, but Frederick managed to hide in the cornfield where the corn was high. From there he made it to the woods. Hiding all day, he met a slave who had a free wife about four miles away. It being Saturday, he was on his way to see her and took Frederick along, even though the act of aiding a disobedient fellow slave would have brought the man thirty-nine lashes. They had a long talk, and the older slave, "a true African," gave him a certain root which, if he would carry it "always on the right side," would make it impossible for any white man to whip him. Skeptical but carrying the root, Frederick went back on the Sunday morning, having rested well. Covey, who was ready to go to church, spoke to him rather kindly, asking him to drive the pigs home.

Monday morning came and with it the order to rub and feed the horses. In the stable Frederick was met by Covey carrying a long rope with which he attempted to tie Frederick's legs. Suddenly the resolve to fight was born in Frederick, who had observed that those slaves easiest to whip received most whippings. He felt he had listened too long to white religious folks telling him to be humble and obedient. "My hands were no longer tied by religion," he said later. Now he used them—

as a man, refusing to be treated this way any longer. He seized the astonished and suddenly trembling Covey by the throat. Covey called for help but, when his cousin Bill Hughes came running, Frederick kicked him hard in the ribs. Hughes doubled over with pain, his fighting spirit knocked out. Covey and Frederick spent another couple of hours fighting, Frederick demanding not to be treated like a beast. He knew that the penalty for going against his master like this, according to state law, could be death, having his body quartered, his head cut off and set up in a prominent place as a warning. But he took the risk, any risk, because he couldn't take his life as it was any longer. The other slaves would not come to Covey's aid—suddenly they were all busy at work somewhere else.

This battle was the turning point in his career as a slave. It reawakened a sense of his manhood. People began to whisper that, if anyone wanted to whip this slave, they would have to kill him first. Although Covey had several opportunities, and even provocation, during the next six months, he never attempted to whip Frederick again.

In the next four years, although involved in several fights, Frederick was not whipped once.

In a cartoon titled "Like Meets Like," abolitionist Garrison (right) is shown shaking hands with South Carolina's secessionist Keitt. South Carolina was the first state to secede from the Union.

Why did Covey not call the constables and take Frederick to the public whipping post? The simplest explanation is probably that he didn't want to ruin his reputation as a first-rate overseer and unmatched Negro-breaker. To admit that he couldn't handle a boy of sixteen would have hurt his reputation immensely.

On Christmas Day 1834, Frederick's service to Covey ended. During the Christmas holidays no work was required except feeding and caring for the stock. It was deemed a disgrace for a slave not to get drunk at Christmas! Any slave who would go on working rather than partying was thought to have rejected a favor from his master. A man who had not saved up for whiskey was considered lazy.

This was an effective means of holding down the spirit of insurrection. The Christmas holidays served as a safety valve; it was a gross fraud, passing for benevolence but in actuality making the slaves sink into dissipation and self-hatred, meant to give them a feeling of disgust for freedom. There were bets on which slave could drink the most. When the holidays ended, the slaves staggered up from the filth and the drunken stupor, almost glad to get back to the fields again.

The method was used in other areas. For

example, if a slave loved molasses and stole some, his master would buy a large quantity of molasses and, with the whip ready, force the slave to eat until he felt sick of even hearing the word molasses.

In January 1835, Frederick was sent to a Mr. Freeland, quite a different sort from Mr. Covey. He had fits of bad humor but was more open and honest, and he made no pretensions of being religious, religion often covering horrid crimes at this time and place. "Religious slaveholders are the worst. I have ever found them the meanest and basest, the most cruel and cowardly, of all others," Frederick declared, telling about another hirer of slaves as farmhands, a Reverend Hopkins, whose chief boast was his ability to manage slaves. He had a habit of whipping them in advance of their deserving it. Every Monday morning was whipping time, the good Reverend always finding a feeble excuse for doing so. Had the slave perhaps forgotten to pull off his hat at the approach of a white person? Did he answer his master too loudly? Take him down a peg! Or did he break a hoe while hoeing? Whip him!

Mr. Freeland, on the other hand, fed the slaves, gave them time to eat, and only worked them between sunrise and sunset. He gave them good tools. He owned two slaves and hired two more. In these Frederick managed to instill a desire to learn to read and began to devote his and their free time on Sundays to teaching them. A few slaves from neighboring farms came to learn as well. It was necessary to keep the fact well hidden that this group of slaves did not spend Sunday wrestling, boxing, and drinking applejack or whiskey, which were approved activities, but that they were doing something considerably more dangerous: they were learning. The lessons were held at the home of a free black man and often included about forty grown men and women, all taking the risk of thirty-nine lashes for wanting to feed their starved minds.

At the close of the year 1835, Mr. Freeland, expanding his work force, hired Frederick from his master for another year. However, Frederick knew he would rather live upon free land than with Freeland, even if the latter was a good master, relatively speaking. Approaching manhood, he resolved that the year 1836 would not pass without him attempting to secure his liberty.

He spoke of his plans with those he trusted, and they were ready to hear and ready to act, if a feasible plan could be worked out. All were aware that even getting away without being caught meant living forever in the fear of being returned to slavery. Yet they wanted to try. They wanted to go north. They knew nothing about Canada. Their knowledge of the North extended no farther than New York.

The dangers of their choice were real indeed. But what did they have to lose? To starve to death literally and symbolically in slavery or to drown, to be torn to pieces by bloodhounds, to be overtaken by slave hunters, to be shot on the spot or brought back to even harder bondage. Frederick resolved that he would prefer death to hopeless slavery forever.

Finally five other men were committed to the classically simple escape attempt; although the youngest, Frederick became the planner and leader. They resolved to steal a large log canoe and paddle directly up Chesapeake Bay on the Saturday night before Easter. Arriving at a point seventy or eighty miles from where they lived, they would set the canoe adrift and walk, following the North Star until getting beyond the limits of Maryland to Pennsylvania. The reason for the water route was that they hoped to be taken for fishermen rather than runaway slaves. Anyone with a white face could stop them at any time and subject them to questions.

Frederick wrote false attestations for each one, claiming to be William Hamilton and

made, and all letters
...ms of the paper are to
... General Agent.
... less than one square in-
...— one square for $1.00.
American, Massachusetts,
...chigan Anti-Slavery So-
...eive subscriptions for The

...lemen constitute the Finan-
...ot responsible for any of the
...:—Francis Jackson, Ed-
Philbrick, and Wendell

...GARRISON, Editor. Our Country is the W...

...IX. NO. 46. BOSTON, FRIDA...

OPPRESSION.

...Boston Post.

...F THE BLACK AND
...REPUBLICANS.

...er of the signs of the times
... there exists a perfect under-
...pose of co-operation between
...osition which seeks by politi-
...possession of the government,
...which is striving to consum-
...ies outside and in defiance of
...gh these two divisions osten-
...t means, and approach the

vention of judge or jury. He was *a villenous pirate and assassin*, and was therefore *entitled to no trial at law*. We believed at the first, and we still more firmly believe now, that it would have been better and wiser in all respects, if Gov. Wise had given him the swift benefit of *a drum-head court-martial*. In that event, no sympathy for him would have been excited in the North, for he would have had no opportunity of making *incendiary speeches for effect*, and, consequently, nothing of the character of the hero or the martyr would have attached to him, even in the estimation of Garrison and Wendell Phillips.

We, therefore, agree fully with our contemporary of the Fredericksburg News in the opinion, that the absurd and horrid nonsense about Gov. Wise's

PHILLIPS'S BROOKLYN LECT...

Wendell Phillips, safe in Boston, is res...
John Brown, incarcerated at Charlesto...
such men as Wendell Phillips is the blood...
and his five associates; and, though h...
villany at present, death may yet unnerv...
and he, too, may cry out '*peccavi!*' as p...
has just done.

What means the applause that greete...
son of Phillips in Brooklyn? What is ...
to understand from such an exhibition o...
tion? Is this the government of two peo...
ferent in our sentiments of right and w...
are in our institutions? When an impuc...
drel, avowing himself 'not a citizen,' a...
one of the States of the confederacy is ...

The most important abolitionist newspaper was the Liberator, *published by William Lloyd Garrison. Upon arriving in the North, Douglass read the paper avidly because it voiced many of his own thoughts and feelings.*

granting the specific slave permission to go to Baltimore for the Easter holidays. They were not headed for Baltimore; these papers were only to protect them while on the bay.

Fears mounted. Frederick spoke every day and every night with the others, dispelling fears, doubts, and indecision; inspiring them, assuring them that the time was as right as it would ever be. Only one, the oldest of them, withdrew after having had an ominous dream in which he had seen Frederick "in the claws of a huge bird, surrounded by a large number of birds of all colors and sizes."

ERATOR.

—William

ur Countrymen are all Mankind. J. B. YERR

NOVEMBER 18, 1859. WHOLE N

SELECTIONS.

EMERSON ON COURAGE.

Extract from the lecture of Ralph Waldo Emerson at the Tremont Temple, Boston, Tuesday evening, 8th instant:—

Courage is of many kinds—Scientific, Temperamental, Ideal. It consists in the conviction that they with whom you contend are no more than you. It is said courage is common, but the immense esteem in which it is held proves this to be an error. Animal resistance, the instinct of the male when cornered, is no doubt common; but the pure article,

gallows glorious like the cross. (Prolonged and enthusiastic applause.)

But 'wisdom is justified of her children.' Valor pays rents as well as lands. A noble cause begets love and confidence, and has a sure reward. High courage, a power of will superior to events, makes a band of union between enemies. If Gov. Wise be a superior man, and inasmuch as he is a superior man, he distinguishes his captive John Brown.

As they confer, they understand each other swiftly; each respects the other, and if opportunity allowed, they would prefer each other's society to that of their former companions. Enemies become affectionate; become aware that they are nearer alike than any other two, and if circumstances did not

The Saturday morning of April 2, whose night was chosen for the escape, arrived. Frederick woke up with a strange premonition that they had been betrayed. As he worked in the field, spreading manure, he became more and more certain of this.

When he came up to the house for breakfast, he was told that some men wanted to see him. He went inside, and two constables seized him, lashing his hands closely together. They tied the hands of another slave, John. Yet another of the five, Henry, entered—and refused to cross his hands to be tied. The constables pulled out pistols. "Shoot me," said Henry. "You can't kill me but once. Shoot, shoot—and be damned! *I won't be tied!*" With a sweeping stroke he dashed the pistol from the hand of each constable. After a brief fight, they managed to overpower and tie him.

The mother of Mr. Freeland came to the door, calling Frederick a yellow devil and accusing him of instigating the escape attempt.

While the slaves were brought to St. Michael's, they chewed up and swallowed the passes Frederick had written to leave no tangible evidence of their plan. The words "Own nothing!" were passed between them. When they reached St. Michael's, all denied that they had been planning to run away. "We were quietly at work!"

They were thrown into jail, three of them in one cell, two in another. Slave traders showed up quickly to look them over, taunting them, talking about the Deep South and how slaves were treated there, but right after Easter, Master Thomas and Mr. Freeland came and took four of them out of jail, leaving Frederick in his cell. They had decided that he was the driving force behind the escape attempt and intended to sell him as a warning to all others.

For some reason, and to Frederick's utter astonishment, Captain Thomas Auld, his master, came and freed him a week later, although simultaneously announcing his intention to send him to a friend in Alabama. For an equally unexplained reason, he did not carry out his threat but sent him back to Baltimore, to live again with Hugh Auld and to learn a trade. One reason for this decision was probably that neither he nor other white slaveholders wanted to keep a slave who could read and write among the plantation slaves. His learning made him dangerous. Better to send him to the city, holding out a hope that, if he behaved himself and learned a trade, he would be set free one day. Perhaps when he turned twenty-five....

Thus, after an absence of three years and one month, Frederick Bailey returned to Baltimore, where he was hired out to a ship builder to learn how to caulk. In actuality, he was now at the beck and call of about seventy-five men, all of whom he was to regard as his masters. Their word was to be his law. "Fred, do this!" "Fred, do that!" "Fred, come here!" All day long.

After eight months, calamity struck. Black and white carpenters (many of the blacks freedmen) had been working together without any great problem. All at once, the white carpenters refused to work with free colored workmen, fearing that this would lead to fewer opportunities of employment for poor white men, such as the increasing number of Irish immigrants. Even the white apprentices picked up on this, resorting to name-calling and declaring that all workers of color should be killed "before they took over the country." They started attacking blacks at every opportunity, and Frederick always fought back. Although he, now over six feet tall and strong from working in the fields, could take them on one on one, he had no chance when they came in groups, armed with sticks, stones, and heavy handspikes. This resulted in his being badly beaten up and almost losing his left eye from a mean kick. At least fifty white ship-carpenters witnessed this uneven fight, doing nothing.

He went back home, and both Master Hugh and his wife Sophia were enraged that he had been attacked by a gang of brutes. Her old gentleness was momentarily awakened, and she washed and bound his face. Even Hugh Auld tried to get the attackers arrested, but nothing could be done unless one white man would step forward and testify. The testimony of a thousand colored people would not have been sufficient to arrest anyone. No whites came forward; those who may have felt sympathy for Frederick did not have the courage to do anything for fear of being called by that,

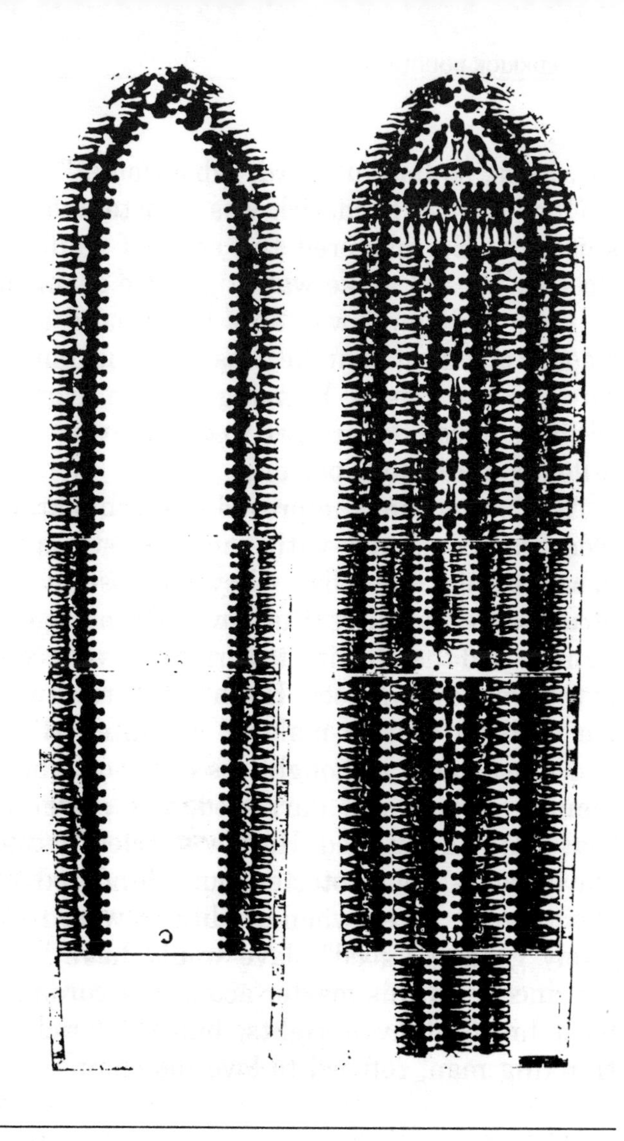

In order to maximize their profits, slave traders packed the slaves into the ships as tightly as possible, knowing that many of them would not survive the long trip across the Atlantic to America.

to whites, so hateful word, “abolitionist!”

Once healed, Frederick was sent to another shipyard. He mastered the craft of caulking (to stop up and make watertight the seams of a boat’s hull) and was able to demand good wages, meaning that he was of some importance to his master, bringing him an average of six to seven dollars per week—he was paid a dollar and a half per day.

As his conditions improved, the thoughts of freedom awakened with renewed strength. When things were bad, they got lost in his struggle to keep alive. But now, earning a good living—and then having to turn over every cent of that money to Master Hugh—they returned. He realized that to make a contented slave, you must make a thoughtless one, one whose mental visions are darkened, his power of reasoning annihilated. He saw too clearly that slaves were not protected but plundered by their owners, even when conditions were relatively good. A “good” slave would have been convinced that his master acted in accordance with his God-given rights, but Frederick, a thinking man, refused to love his chains.

Both Henry Ward Beecher (left) and Harriet Beecher Stowe (right) were staunch abolitionists. Beecher was a prominent minister, and Harriet wrote the novel, Uncle Tom's Cabin, *which may have been the single most important antislavery tract.*

UNCLE TOM'S CABI
UNCLE TOM & EVA.

Chapter Six

Breaking Loose

WHEN FREDERICK Douglass told about planning his escape and finally succeeding, he was carefully omitting many important facts. His book *Narrative of the Life of Frederick Douglass, An American Slave* (with the proud three words below his picture, "Written by Himself"), was published at the Anti-Slavery Office in Boston in the year 1845. Slavery still existed in many states, and one careless word could have endangered others. It would also have induced greater vigilance on the part of slaveholders, and the last thing he wanted to do was close a door that might make it possi-

Uncle Tom's Cabin *was an immediate success in the North, and the people of the South became highly affronted by its publication. The book was adapted as a play, which was performed throughout the North.*

ble for another slave to escape.

In that connection he criticized the way the "underground railroad" was conducted, saying that it was so open that it ought to be called the "upperground railroad." While ever honoring the good men and women for their daring and applauding them for subjecting themselves to persecution by openly declaring their participation in aiding runaways, he noted, "They do much towards enlightening the masters. I would keep the merciless slaveholder profoundly ignorant of the means of flight adopted by the slave.... Let him be left to feel his way in the dark; let darkness commensurate with his crime hover over him; and let him feel that at every step he takes, running in pursuit of the flying bondman, he is running the frightful risk of having his hot brains dashed out by an invisible agency. Let us render the tyrant no aid."

In the early part of 1838, however, Frederick was still a slave, a restless slave with a fire burning inside. Why should he, at the end of every week, hand over to his master the money he had earned by his heavy labor? When he made six dollars, his master sometimes handed him six cents—*to encourage him!* The few cents probably eased the man's conscience and made him feel like an honorable kind of robber.

Unceasingly, Frederick was looking for means of escape.

In the spring, when his actual owner, Hugh's brother Thomas, came to Baltimore, Frederick asked for permission to hire himself out and then pay a certain amount for room and board. Thomas must have sensed something because he told him that, should he run away, no efforts would be spared to catch him. "Be obedient," said the man. "If you would be happy, make no plans for the future." If Frederick kept behaving himself, he would be well taken care of. Thomas Auld, like most slaveholders, wanted his slave to depend solely on him, the master, for his happiness.

Two months later, Master Thomas having long since left, Frederick applied to Master Hugh for the same privilege. Hugh did not know that his brother had refused the request. After some reflection Hugh agreed: Frederick could seek employment wherever he was able, make his contracts, pay Hugh three dollars a week, and pay for his own clothing and caulking tools. This made Frederick's regular expenses about six dollars a week. Could he not come up with that sum every week, for whatever reason, he would have to give up his privilege. The agreement meant that Hugh did not need to look after him any more but would get his money every week. He had all the benefits of slaveholding without cost, while Frederick had to endure being a slave and at the same time had to worry about where to find work, the same as a free man.

Still and all, it meant taking on responsibility, and he saw that as a definite step toward freedom.

He worked hard from May until August, managing to put away a few cents here and there. He also went to a secret debating club for free blacks, "The East Baltimore Mutual Improvement Society," where slaves were actually not allowed. He began to speak there as well as at some religious meetings for blacks. At one social get-together, he met a free woman named Anna Murray, employed as a domestic. She was a few years older than he, a dark, quiet, hardworking girl who could neither read nor write but who was more practical than the young impulsive man. The two became engaged. She encouraged him to pursue his feeling for music, and his lifelong love affair with the violin began.

In August his work privilege was revoked—he had been late paying the weekly amount due to having attended a meeting Saturday night, returning late, and figuring he could pay the money Sunday morning. When he came to do so, Master Hugh was flaming mad. Discovering that Frederick had gone about ten miles out of the city to attend a meeting, his anger increased. Thinking it over, he must have realized that he was losing control over this independent young man, and he forbade him to hire out his time any longer, correctly assuming that the next step would be escape. Instead they would return to the old system of Frederick working and bringing all the money home to him.

Frederick decided to retaliate. The following week he did not do one scrap of work. Came Saturday night, when Hugh called upon him to bring the money, Frederick told him he had no wages; he had done no work. Hugh came close to striking him then, but perhaps he saw something in the smoldering eyes, something that promised that this one would not take well to being hit but would give back, blow for blow.

Realizing that things might get stricter after this, even to the point of his being sold down South, Frederick decided on his exact day of escape, September 3, three weeks and one day hence.

He went out on Monday and found work, worked hard all week, and brought home between eight and nine dollars. This pleased his master—which was the idea. Frederick's main aim was to remove any suspicions harbored by Hugh Auld, wanting him to think that Frederick had finally accepted his condition in the days and weeks right before his escape. The second week Frederick brought him again his full wages, which pleased the master so that he handed over twenty-five cents with the words, "Make good use of it."

Frederick experienced inner turmoil as he prepared to leave good friends in Baltimore behind, most of whom he would be separated from forever. In addition, there was the dread and apprehension of failure, with its dire consequences. Failure would seal his fate as a slave forever.

On September 3, 1838, he left his chains and, aided by uncommon luck, succeeded in reaching New York without getting caught.

He was free at last but homeless, poor, with insecurity and loneliness in his soul, until he met the man named David Ruggles, "whose vigilance, kindness and perseverance I shall never forget." Although they were watched and hemmed in on every side, Ruggles managed to get Frederick out of New York along with his brand-new wife, Anna.

Life in New Bedford began for the former slave Frederick Bailey alias Stanley alias

The slave of a Missouri doctor who was serving in the U.S. Army, Dred Scott, though not badly treated by his master, sought to acquire his freedom after accompanying his owner for long periods in Illinois and Wisconsin, both free states.

Frederick Johnson alias—finally—Frederick Douglass.

Life in the North was partly a disappointment, partly an eye-opener. Knowing that the northern people did not own slaves, he had supposed that this meant they were poor, as the non-slaveholders of the South were poor. Somehow he had ingested the opinion that there could be no wealth and little refinement without slaves. He had believed that the people of the North would not only be poor but also rough and uncultivated, knowing nothing of the ease and luxury of southern slaveholders' lives.

The first thing he did was visit the wharves to see how the shipping business was faring, since that was where he would expect to earn his living. He was surprised to see large, fine ships, as well as granite warehouses of great size and filled with the comforts of life. Everybody seemed to be working but without the constant cursing that went on in the South. He saw no men being whipped. He went for a stroll through town, seeing churches, beautiful houses, and fine gardens. There were few dilapidated houses with half-naked children and barefooted women. Well, but those were the white folks—what about the blacks, then being called the "colored people?"

Many of them were escaped slaves, and he found that several who had been free less than seven years had bought their own houses, often finer than those of many slaveholders in Maryland. The couple who had taken him in, Nathan Johnson and his wife, were but one example. Their house was beautiful, good food was served, several newspapers were read; in every way their life was better than "nine-tenths of the slaveholders in Talbot county of Maryland." Mr. Johnson was a working man, as was his wife; both were high-spirited and determined.

Another thing that impressed Frederick was the brotherhood existing among blacks. There had been an argument between a black man and a recently arrived fugitive slave, and the former had been heard threatening to inform on the latter. A meeting was called, led by an old, religious gentleman, to which the man who had threatened to betray a brother was invited. Whereupon the old man told those present that a betrayer was among them, and he recommended for the young men to take him outside and kill him! A few set out to do so but were held back by others; the man escaped and was not seen again in New Bedford. No one else threatened to betray an escapee.

On Monday, Frederick Douglass dressed for work. Seeing a pile of coal in front of a house, he went over and was employed to shovel it into the cellar, after which the lady of the house put two silver half-dollars in his hand, the first money he had earned that he could keep. Three days after his arrival, Frederick was working at stowing a sloop with a load of oil—hard work, but he was his own master and did not mind at all. The reward for the work was all his own. No master of any kind stood ready to rob him of his earnings.

He tried for a job in his profession as a caulker, but even here strong prejudice existed among the white caulkers. Other work was available, however: he sawed wood, shoveled coal, carried wood, swept chimneys, rolled oil casks, dug cellars, removed rubbish from backyards, scoured cabins. During the winter he worked as a waiter but liked that less than the hard manual work. His last place of employment in New Bedford was at Richmond's brass foundry. Thus passed his first three years as a free man.

His wife, Anna, worked in people's houses, serving and washing. On June 24, 1839, their first child was born, a girl whom they named Rosetta. The following year, on October 2, 1840, their son Lewis Henry was born.

At this time, a newspaper called the *Liberator* was published weekly. It became Frederick's meat and drink, setting his soul on fire. Here he read the opinions of people who sympathized with his brethren in bonds, who denounced slaveholders, who attacked those who wished to uphold the institution of slavery.

Soon he understood the principles, measures, and spirit of the antislavery reform movement. He went to antislavery meetings. He remained mostly quiet because he felt that what he wanted to say was said better by others, although he did speak up at smaller meetings with only black people present.

His zeal for religion had been weakened by what he had experienced in Maryland. Now he felt that the Lord had brought him out of bondage and, expecting things to be different, he went to the Elm Street Methodist Church, full of hope to be treated as a man and a brother. "These Christian people would have none of this unholy feeling against color, I thought." The result was "most humiliating." The white members went forward to the altar by the bench-full. When the preacher had made sure that all his whites had been served, the turn came for the blacks. "I went out, and have never been in that church since," he said. He tried other churches, with the same result.

Various kinds of sailing ships were used in the slave trade—schooners, sloops, and snows being most common. Interestingly, it was the seafaring trade, which had brought the slaves to America, that ultimately proved to be the means of escape from

slavery for many. Some even took to becoming sailors or whalers because it was much easier to elude the slave catchers by a life at sea. By trade, Frederick Douglass was a ship's caulker, and in his escape to the North he traveled part of the way by boat.

At a revival meeting, a deacon said what was often heard from bus drivers, doorkeepers, and others, "We don't allow niggers in here." He then joined the African M.E. Zion Church but left it soon because the pastor refused to give notice of antislavery meetings. Occasionally Frederick Douglass would officiate as a lay-preacher in a little schoolhouse on Second Street.

He read voraciously, nailing up a newspaper in the foundry so he could look at it while he worked. He read poetry, he read science and philosophy, he read the Bible, but he read the *Liberator* even more devoutly and went to lectures, among others to one (on April 15, 1839) given by William Lloyd Garrison, the editor of the paper. "In him there was no contradiction between the speech and its speaker, but absolute sympathy and oneness," Frederick wrote to a friend.

By 1840, the Pennsylvania Abolition Society had been formed, books had been printed against slavery, and laws to check its increase had been passed. Vermont had prohibited the wicked institution already in 1777, and her example was followed throughout the North. Demands for immediate emancipation had been published, but most seemed to strive and wish for gradual measures, and before 1830 the general character of the controversy was peaceable. Then, partly through Garrison's demand for "immediate and unconditional emancipation," things changed. What has been called "the Martyr Age of the United States" began. Garrison was imprisoned for seven weeks as a result of his demands.

The first issue of his *Liberator* had been published on January 1, 1831, after which a reward had been offered anyone to kidnap the editor. A Connecticut lady had been put into prison for "trying to educate colored girls." An academy for colored people in New Hampshire was dragged from its foundations by a hundred yoke of oxen, all in accordance with a vote at a town meeting. Destruction of black people's houses, murder, riots, mob actions, all had been going on in the years before Frederick Douglass arrived in New Bedford.

Chapter Seven

A Speaker is Born

FREDERICK DOUGLASS had gone to a meeting where he had heard not only Garrison but other leading abolitionists, which led him to take a holiday in order to attend a big anti-slavery convention at the Atheneum Hall on the island of Nantucket on Wednesday, August 11, 1841. One William Coffin, who had heard Douglass say a few words at a meeting of blacks in New Bedford, urged him to speak up. He was reluctant, still feeling himself a slave and not quite having gotten rid of his fear of speaking in front of white people. In the end, he did heed Coffin's urgings, standing up for

---

Initially the Civil War was over the issue of whether states could secede from the union, though slavery was one of the most important issues that divided North from South. Douglass pressed for Lincoln to make it the *principal issue, which he did.*

a few moments, "trembling in every limb" but speaking with surprising ease. Although afterwards he said that this speech, his first in front of a mixed audience, "is about the only one I ever made of which I do not remember a single connected sentence." The listeners, however, remembered his words about his life as a slave and were so impressed that they asked him to open the next day's session.

Thus began his role as a spokesman for his oppressed brethren. Everyone who heard him knew that here was a man, speaking from his heart, with sharp intelligence and true passion. Nobody could forget Frederick Douglass once they had been reached by his rich, melodious voice, his enunciation excellent as he spoke with wit, arguments, sarcasm, pathos, and honesty. For many, this was the first time they had a chance to hear firsthand what it was like to be a slave, what inhuman hardships slavery put upon fellow beings. He awakened and strengthened a hatred for slavery in his audiences. "Flinty hearts were pierced, and cold ones melted by his eloquence," wrote a reporter.

Speaking out, even in a state where slavery was illegal, was a dangerous thing for him to do: he was still a fugitive slave according to federal law. His former master would have the legal right to send a slave hunter in to bring him back in chains.

He was approached by the American Anti-Slavery Society; they wanted him to be their agent, traveling to various towns and cities in the northern part of the United States, speaking to audiences about his personal experiences, making a plea for the end of slavery; for his work he would be paid four hundred and fifty dollars a year. He was unwilling to accept the post at first, not only because of the dangers involved but because he distrusted his own ability. In the end, he accepted, knowing that his voice was needed, and he kept impressing and arousing audiences everywhere, one way or another. Many times he was met with hostility, even attacked by armed thugs, by those who wanted no change.

The editor of the *Liberator*, William Lloyd Garrison, was a white man. (Most of the leaders of the abolitionist movement were white, not because there weren't black leaders but because even those liberated whites still had a tendency to see blacks if not as inferior at least as children who needed time to grow up and catch up.) Garrison, who compared Douglass to Spartacus, the rebel gladiator, had been present at that first speech of Douglass's and was instrumental in getting him more speaking engagements, during which he also was to take subscriptions to the *Liberator* as well as to another newspaper called the *Anti-Slavery Standard*.

"Douglass was cut out for a hero," wrote the newspaper *Herald of Freedom*, saying he had "the heart to conceive, the head to contrive, and the hand to execute."

At this time some free blacks had moved to Liberia, into the area in Africa that had been established in 1822. Douglass did not believe that blacks should be forced to return to Africa as part of a colonization scheme that some advocated. He felt that by now the real home of black Americans was the United States of America.

Douglass and Garrison shared this view as well as the strong conviction that the way to end slavery was to educate people. "If we can convince them of the evil in what they are doing, they will change," Garrison said about the slaveholders. Neither man believed in violent uprising as a tool of change.

They kept trying to reach people through the churches; these, however, refused to take a stand against slavery. Douglass would sometimes sing a parody on a familiar hymn (about being saved from a burning hell, and dwelling with Immanuel in heavenly union), to wit:

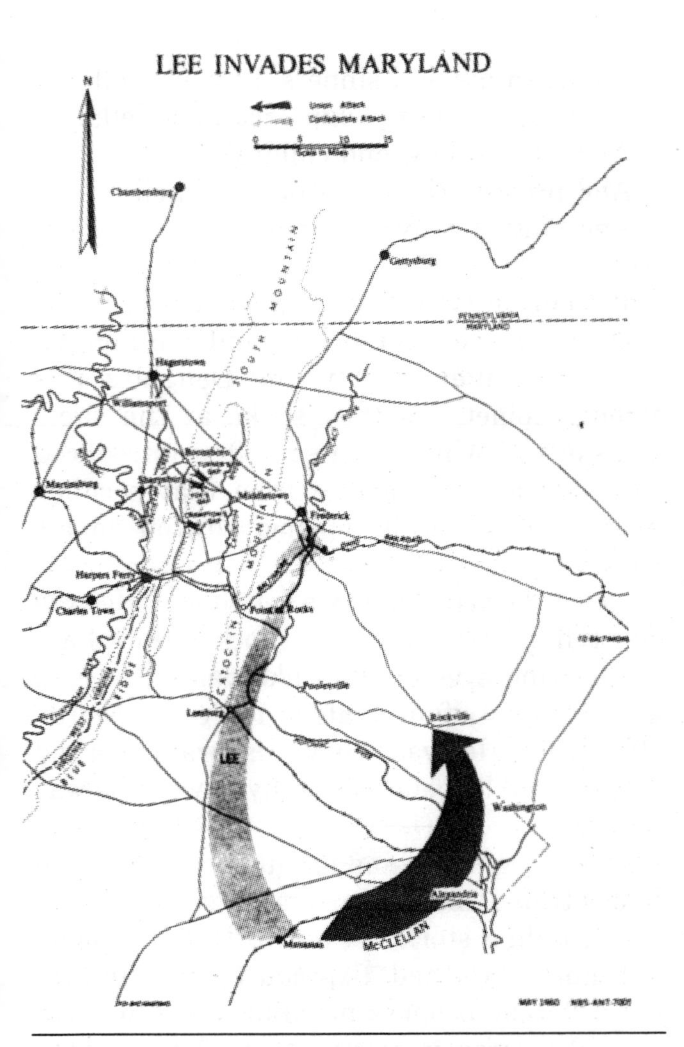

After the Second Battle of Manassas, a Confederate victory, General Robert E. Lee decided to invade Maryland, hoping the people of the North would become disillusioned with the war after experiencing the horror of battles on their own territory.

Come, saints and sinners, hear me tell,
How pious priests whip Jack and Nell,
And women buy, and children sell,
And preach all sinners down to hell,
And sing of heavenly union.

It went on for many satirical verses.

Garrison was outspoken and passionate, and his influence on young Douglass was strong. Sometimes they spoke at the same occasions at which Garrison often introduced Douglass as "a graduate from that peculiar institution, with his diploma written on his back."

Douglass kept having a lot to say. He was also tall, handsome, with a shock of thick hair, penetrating eyes, a voice like dark molasses, and an electrifying talent for using words effectively. He was witty, his brain worked quickly, and he believed totally in what he was saying.

In the beginning and for quite some time he concentrated mainly on his personal experiences, telling stories of horror but also using rich humor. He had a special flair for imitating different people (including white preachers). Why was it so necessary for a former slave, still a fugitive, to stand up and tell what was going on in the slave states? Didn't everyone know? Wasn't it evident to people, at least in the North, that you should not keep people in chains, that it was wrong to *own* other human beings?

One must remember that the proslavery propaganda was strong and clever, describing slaves as happy, singing, childlike creatures who loved their masters' families like their own, who lived in total security, who were well-treated and didn't have to work at all as hard as a lot of white labor in the North. Most had never heard a slave's version. As a matter of fact, many had never heard a black man speak. Douglass told them the truth, and he helped to defeat a measure that would have given voting rights to poor whites while denying the same rights to blacks. He was noting more and more that, while a lot of white people wished the black people well, their attitude was still paternalistic in nature; in other words, they kept existing within the framework of white supremacy.

Toward the end of 1842, Douglass became involved in the case of a fugitive slave found in Boston and about to be returned to his master. Douglass's speeches and letters to newspapers resulted in citizens of Boston buying the man from his owner. The following year Douglass went to visit what was at the time the American West (Indiana, Ohio, Illinois, etc.), sang songs about abolition of slavery in town squares, was hit by eggs and stones, nearly beaten to death at one time, but was also well received by fascinated listeners. Slowly, the seed was being sown—and Frederick Douglass was tireless and highly influential in shaping and reshaping public opinion and increasing awareness.

He won more and more admirers, black and white, although there were some who feared a black man with such eloquence and intelligence. At one time or another, he was even advised to "keep a little of the plantation speech" so as not to scare people away! "It's best you do not seem too learned," he was told. Even within the abolitionist movement, he was at times cautioned to keep his speeches to his own experiences and not, as he was doing increasingly, deal with abstract issues, heretofore only dealt with by white leaders of the movement, such as Garrison and others. "Give us the facts, we will take care of the philosophy."

Rumors spread that a man with such command of words and appearing as confident and cultured could not possibly have been a slave, growing up without any education. This was largely what led him to write his first book,

Narrative of the Life of Frederick Douglass, An American Slave, which was published in May 1845.

The preface to the book was written by William Lloyd Garrison, who told of his first meeting with Douglass, of hearing him speak ("the extraordinary emotion it excited in my own mind"), of the latter's "virtuous traits of character..., ever-abiding remembrance of those who are in bonds...," attesting to the fact that Douglass had indeed written his own narrative "rather than to employ someone else." He ends it:

"Reader! are you with the man-stealers in sympathy and purpose, or on the side of their down-trodden victims? If with the former, then are you the foe of God and man. If with the latter, what are you prepared to do and dare in their behalf? Be faithful, be vigilant, be untiring in your efforts to break every yoke, and let the oppressed go free. Come what may—cost what it may—inscribe on the banner which you unfurl to the breeze, as your religious and political motto—"NO COMPROMISE WITH SLAVERY! NO UNION WITH SLAVEHOLDERS!"

The book also contains a letter from Wendell Phillips, the Harvard-graduated reformer and orator, addressed to Frederick Douglass, "My

The Union army was better supplied with materiel for war than the Confederacy, having the industries to make the rifles, cannons, and ammunition, but the Confederacy

Dear Friend." He says among other things that "I shall read your book with trembling for you. Some years ago, when you were beginning to

had the better military leaders, the experienced generals who knew how to win battles. Eventually, however, the Union leaders gained experience, and the tide turned.

tell me your real name and birthplace, you may remember I stopped you, and preferred to remain ignorant of all."

Chapter Eight

All True Reforms are Kindred

DOUGLASS'S AUTOBIOGRAPHY, a document telling the terrible truth about what it is to be a slave and also a tribute to the dignity and courage of a human being, became an almost immediate best-seller. By 1848, eleven thousand copies had been sold. His name became known all over the nation and in large parts of the rest of the world, as it was quickly translated into German, Dutch, and French. In England, it was into its ninth edition.

But Wendell Phillips and others were right: his old master could lawfully send slave hunters after him, and by now he would not

With the fall of Richmond, Virginia, the capital of the Confederate States, the citizens packed what possessions they could and quickly fled. The Union army blew up the Confederate arsenals and set fire to the city.

be difficult to find. So on Saturday, August 16, 1845, after seven years in constant danger of arrest, a danger that had increased now when he had published both the name and the address of his slave master, Douglass set out for England, which had freed all slaves within the British Empire by 1838 as a result of a gradual emancipation law of 1833.

The Douglass family at this time included four children—Rosetta, 6; Lewis, 5; Frederick, 3; and Charles, still under a year old. Anna, who worked in a shoe factory, earned enough to support the family while her husband went away to Europe, taking the steamship *Cambria* across the Atlantic. He had to sail steerage on the ship due to his skin color, but he was also invited by the captain to the saloon deck to give a lecture on slavery. There were some young men ("proslavery grumblers") aboard who were angered by this and made ugly threats to throw Douglass overboard, but the captain kept them in order by threatening to put them in irons. In this he was assisted by several passengers, especially a high-spirited Irishman.

For nearly two years, Douglass traveled around England. Big crowds came to hear him, and people welcomed him to their homes. He wrote to William Lloyd Garrison: "I breathe and lo! The chattel becomes man. I gaze around in vain for one who will question my equal humanity, claim me as a slave, or offer me an insult."

When he visited Ireland, where they called him "the black O'Connell" (after one of their folk heroes), he decided to abstain from alcohol, still bearing in mind how slave owners had encouraged the slaves to drink themselves into a stupor during any time off from work, and seeing how alcohol enslaved many. He became also involved in the fight for Irish independence, identifying with the desire of the Irish to be their own men, saying, "All true reforms are kindred."

After about a year, Garrison joined Douglass, and the two traveled and lectured together. Among other things they involved themselves in a campaign against the Free Church of Scotland, partly funded by slaveholders in America of Scottish descent.

Most of Douglass's lectures centered on slavery. He told that, in Virginia, blacks could be executed for no less than seventy-one crimes. (Only three crimes would lead to execution of whites.)

Many tried to encourage him to stay in England, to be truly free of the fear of chains. Although he loved his new life ("I find myself not treated as a color, but as a man"), he missed his family, and he knew that his black brethren, three million of his fellow creatures, were still in bondage. His British friends took up a collection and bought Frederick for $711.66 from Hugh Auld (to whom Thomas Auld had transferred the title of ownership). Auld signed the papers, and on December 12, 1846, at 10:00 A.M., Frederick Douglass ceased to be a chattel and was a free man in the eyes of the law, at approximately twenty-eight years of age.

Douglass appreciated what his friends had done, even though he did not acknowledge the right of any man to own another man. "I have as much right to sell Hugh Auld as Hugh Auld has to sell me," he joked, recognizing Auld only as a kidnapper, not as his master.

In the spring of 1847 he took the steamship *Cambria* back to the United States. Reunited with his family and friends, he decided to found and edit a new newspaper, mainly funded by supporters in England, who had sent him five hundred pounds to use as he chose. The givers of the money even stated, "If at any time he should consider it advisable to establish a newspaper of his own, the capital so invested shall be available for that purpose."

Garrison and others opposed his plan, saying there was no room for another antislavery journal and that Douglass was better fitted for speaking than writing. Feeling that he owed Garrison a debt, Douglass let the matter rest for a while. This protest of some abolitionists in combination with their earlier cautions not to appear too learned might have been an indication of the hesitation of even the most liberal minds at the time to accept him as his own man and their equal, a fact that might also have occurred to Frederick Douglass.

In the fall he pursued the idea of his own newspaper again. He decided not to have its headquarters in New England, where Garrison's *Liberator* was published, but rather in Rochester, New York. He moved there with his family, buying a two-story brick house.

He called his newspaper, a weekly, the *North Star* and the first issue saw the light of day on December 3, 1847. It was four pages long. "Right is of no sex—Truth is of no color—God is the Father of us all, and we are all Brethren," he declared on the masthead.

Friends came to work for him, and his children helped to set the type. While the new paper was heralded by many, some of the good people in Rochester did not like the idea of a black newspaper, edited by an ex-slave, being published in their town. The *New York Herald*

On September 5 and 6, 1862, a host of nearly sixty-thousand ragtag Confederate soldiers splashed across the Potomac River at White's Ford, near Leesburg, Virginia, into Maryland. The

Batle of Antietam, or Sharpsburg, was the first invasion of the North by the Confederacy, and it proved to be one of the bloodiest battlefields of the entire war, as well as a northern victory.

even urged the citizens to dump Douglass's printing press in Lake Ontario. However, the town in general was strongly pro-abolitionist, and Douglass rode out the protests.

In his agenda he included a new reform, even more unpopular than abolition: women's suffrage. Several strong leaders in the fight for women's rights associated with Douglass, notably Susan B. Anthony, Lucretia Mott, and Elizabeth Cady Stanton. In July of 1848, a Woman's Rights Convention was held, where a declaration of independence (closely copied from the one adopted by the nation in 1776) was signed by a hundred men and women, and among the names is that of Frederick Douglass. He wrote: "Standing as we do upon the watchtower of human freedom, we cannot be deterred from an expression...to improve and elevate the character of any members of the human family.... Our doctrine is that 'Right is of no sex.' We, therefore, bid the women engaged in this movement our humble God-speed."

He continued his lecture tours, partly to raise money for his newspaper, which couldn't keep up its quality from subscriptions alone. Friends from England remained loyal and helpful; one of these, Julia Griffith, kept raising funds for him and even came over to put

Douglass's finances in order. By 1851 the newspaper was self-supporting, even generating a small profit; by now it was named *Frederick Douglass's Paper*, providing a much needed forum for black writers.

It was published as a weekly until 1860 and then, until 1863, as a monthly. The paper established Frederick Douglass as a force independent of the white abolitionists, including William Loyd Garrison, and his attention was increasingly turned toward black leaders, both a man such as Henry Highland Garnet, who supported blacks going back to Africa, and Charles Remond, an abolitionist. Strong discussions took place between them, discussions that Douglass welcomed because it meant that blacks were beginning to make up their own minds regarding their own future.

"First, the freedom of the blacks in this country, and, second, the elevation of them."

Chapter Nine

Eloquent, Energetic—and Escaping Again

FREDERICK DOUGLASS'S wife, Anna, a hard worker, an excellent housewife, and a good woman who created a close-knit, domestic home life, was completely uneducated. She could not even read. As her husband's mental abilities were honed even more with time and he was being seen by the world as a first-rate writer, thinker, and orator, the intellectual gap between them was rapidly widening. Trying to bridge this gap, he hired a teacher for her but without much success. He always showed her the greatest respect and exacted the same from all others, and he adored their children—

General George McClellan saw the Civil War as an opportunity to advance his own ambitions. It might have been, if he had been willing to fight battles. After Lincoln fired him, McClellan ran—unsuccessfully—for president against Lincoln.

the fifth one, Annie, was born in 1849.

He had many women friends, not the least those in the fight for women's rights, and he did admire educated, strong, outspoken women. Handsome, charming, and articulate as Douglass was, women were attracted to him. Julia Griffith, the British lady, remained in Rochester, even living in the home of the Douglass family, and was constantly at his side. People became used to seeing the tall black man and the white woman going places, often arm in arm. She had become his business manager and ran the newspaper office, set up his lectures, and went with him to various meetings.

There were rumors. There were attacks from people in the Garrison camp, accusing him of creating scandals within the abolitionist movement. To spare him criticism, Julia Griffith moved out of the Douglass home, and, in 1855, she returned to England, although the two of them kept up a lively correspondence for the next forty years.

Douglass and Garrison were by now headed in different directions ideologically. Garrison kept insisting on non-violent ways to change the situation, but Douglass, who had first met the militant white abolitionist John Brown in 1847, was not sure that this would always work. In principle, he believed in the superiority of moral persuasion over political or other action, and in bringing about reforms without resorting to violence. As the 1850s moved on, Douglass became convinced that slavery could not end by peaceful means alone and was encouraging slaves to free themselves by any means available. He kept telling them that people at the bottom have the power of nothing to lose.

A turning point might have been an incident, possibly in Indiana, where a band of rowdy men, armed with pistols and clubs, marched into a lecture hall where he was to speak. They were about to attack Douglass, but one lady, the wife of a local physician, held up her baby in front of him, and he was unharmed. Somewhat later, a battle broke out, and he took active part in it, armed with a stick, having banished his ideas of non-resistance.

At another place, warning was given that Douglass was going to be taken out to be tarred and feathered. One of the abolitionists told Douglass in a whisper about a back door, after which he treated the rapidly advancing men with utmost courtesy. "What can I do for you?" "We want nothing of you. We want that nigger of yours." "Beg your pardon, gentlemen,

Charleston, South Carolina, was the most important port on the South's eastern seaboard. During the Civil War, the Union navy attempted to blockade all southern ports, with an emphasis on Charleston, and for the most part the blockade was successful,

though a few blockade runners did get through. Since the South did not have the kind of industry the North had, it was dependent on obtaining critical supplies from Europe. With trade cut off, it was inevitable the South would lose the war.

but I'm very deaf," said he, who in actuality was hard of hearing. "We want Fred Douglass." "What did you say?" And so it went until Douglass was safely out of the building.

It was proving difficult indeed for Douglass to embrace wholly the doctrine of non-resistance, as he found it increasingly impractical. He also felt that the time was ripe for political reforms—realizing that the North would never fight strongly against slavery if it would mean dividing the country into North and South. This was another difference with Garrison, who was strongly pro-Union. Douglass became increasingly embroiled in politics and was urging his readers to engage in politics as well. He demanded that blacks be given full political and legal rights as American citizens under the Constitution.

He tried to establish a school to train blacks as skilled tradesmen. Harriet Beecher Stowe (who wrote *Uncle Tom's Cabin*, basically an antislavery novel) was helpful in trying to raise money, but even with her assistance he was not able to collect enough to start the trade school.

He worked hard to end segregation in the Rochester school system. His daughter Rosetta, at age nine, had been accepted in a private school kept by a Christian lady. But the little girl was unhappy and he found out why: she was kept in a room by herself, a prisoner on account of her color, not permitted to see or hear the other pupils. His complaints led nowhere; although none of the other children had any objections to Rosetta, one pupil's father had. From then on, Douglass had his children taught at home by a British teacher. (In 1857, the efforts of Douglass and others succeeded—the schools were desegregated.) He opposed all restrictions at theaters, lecture-rooms, and other public places. The influence of his paper and his opinions reached far and wide.

Meanwhile the country was divided. As new areas were taken over by settlers, the opinions on the slave issue were varied. Congress had to try to keep an equal number of free states and slave states. For every slave state admitted to the Union, one free state had to be admitted. Then came California's application, wishing to enter as a free state, which would upset the balance. The Compromise of 1850 gave California statehood, but it also resulted in the Fugitive Slave Act, which gave slave owners more strength in recapturing runaway slaves. Many distinguished Americans of the time objected strongly to this: the American poet and philosopher Ralph Waldo Emerson,

Charles Francis Adams (the son of a president and the grandson of another), John Albion Andrews, the governor of Massachusetts, Lysander Spooner, the philosopher, and others. Forty-seven Massachusetts preachers of all faiths, except the Roman Catholic, spoke up as well, declaring the law unconstitutional and an affront to everyone as it assaulted the rights that are inalienable to American citizens.

A committee of safety and vigilance was formed in Boston, securing the rights of *any* black man from invasion by persons acting under this law. The working group became eighty men, then grew to two hundred and fifty, a good percentage of them black. Over a dozen members of the Boston bar used their legal training to resist, battle, and defy this law.

But in 1854, the Kansas–Nebraska Act was passed, allowing slavery to extend its reach into northern territories of the West. According to this act, the citizens of each new state could vote on whether they wanted slavery or not. The Democrats were trying to appease the southern members, which led to antislavery groups forming the Republican party, and it took the lead in the moral crusade against slavery.

Then in 1857, the Supreme Court made its infamous Dred Scott decision, which in fact declared that slaves were private property, like animals or furniture; if taken into free states by owners, they remained legally bound to them. (Dred Scott was a slave who sued for his freedom, having lived four years in a state where slavery was illegal. The Supreme Court—Chief Justice Roger Taney—said that slaves were not citizens of the United States and therefore "had no right which the white man was bound to respect.")

Douglass became strongly involved in the underground railroad, working to bring runaways to safe places in the North and in Canada. Safe stations were established all the way from places near the North–South border. Douglass's own home was close to the Canadian border and became an important station on the underground railroad. When he came to work in the morning, there were often fugitives sitting on the steps outside his newspaper office. Frequently he and his wife had ten or twelve people hidden in their home.

His wife's contribution in all this should not be underestimated, nor her sense of humor. About this time, she needed to engage a servant, saying to her: "I hope you have no prejudices about color. I have none myself."

On every Fourth of July, Frederick Douglass took the occasion to speak strongly against slavery. "What to the American slave is your Fourth of July?... To him your celebration is a sham..., a thin veil to cover up crimes which would disgrace a nation of savages." Or, "Must I undertake to prove that a slave is a man?... Would you have me argue that man is entitled to liberty? That he is the rightful owner of his own body?"

After the Fugitive Slave Act, requiring citizens to aid the marshals in capturing any runaway, things were harder, and many, many runaways were captured. The revolts at some plantations were generally unsuccessful as well.

The gray-bearded, iron-willed John Brown was a frequent visitor to the Douglass home during the 1850s, advocating militant abolitionism and wanting to start a slave insurrection in the South. This is the man about whom it was said that his stare could force a dog or a cat out of a room. Douglass explained later, "John Brown's plan, as it was then formed in his mind, was very simple, and had much to commend it. It did not, as some suppose, directly contemplate a general uprising among the slaves, and a general slaughter of the slave-masters, but it did contemplate the creation of an armed force, which should constantly act against slavery in the heart of the South."

On Saturday, August 20, 1859, Brown and Douglass met for the last time. Their meeting took place in an old stone quarry on the Conecochege, near the town of Chambersburg, Pennsylvania. Brown's arms and ammunition were stored in that town and were to be moved the same night to Harper's Ferry in northern Virginia, where Brown planned to seize the weapons in the federal armory and hold the citizens hostage while he rounded up slaves in the area, establishing a kind of sanctuary. He had written to Douglass, urging him to come and join him. Douglass had refused, knowing that an attack on federal property would enrage most Americans. The two men talked for hours, Douglass telling Brown that he was going into a steel trap, Brown saying, "Come with me, Douglass, I will defend you with my life." They separated; Douglass went back to Rochester, and John Brown went to Harper's Ferry, from which he would never return.

On October 16, 1859, Brown and his twenty-one men crossed the Potomac and seized Harper's Ferry; the next night Robert E. Lee led federal troops into the town. Brown was captured, two of his sons were killed along with eight other men—and within two months Brown was tried for treason, found guilty, and on December 2, at Charles Town, the hangman's trap was sprung.

Newspaper accounts featured the name of Frederick Douglass, since letters from him had been found in a carpetbag among Brown's belongings. Federal officers were on their way to arrest him in order to bring him to trial in Virginia. Douglass, knowing that he had little chance for a fair trial there, fled to Canada six hours before the marshals arrived. From there he wrote letters, justifying both his flight and his refusal to help Brown. He did not condone the raid on federal property but praised Brown as a "noble old hero."

Toward the end of 1859, Douglass sailed to England for a lecture tour; the British were eager to hear about Harper's Ferry. Douglass declared that "slavery might be put down by honestly carrying out the provisions of the Constitution."

The following spring in May, as he was ready to set out for lectures in France, he received word that his youngest child, Annie ("the light and life of my house"), had died. Heartbroken he decided to go home; by now he had been freed of all charges, the public furor had died down, and John Brown was being spoken of as a martyr for the abolitionist cause. Two who wrote glowingly about him were Henry David Thoreau and Ralph Waldo Emerson. Another contemporary, E.C. Stedman wrote:

> And Old Brown,
> Osawatomie Brown,
> May trouble you more than ever,
> When you've nailed his coffin down!

Douglass spoke frequently about Brown as well. "He saw the evil through no mist, haze, or clouds, but in a broad light of infinite brightness.... His zeal in the cause of freedom was infinitely superior to mine. Mine was as the taper light; his was the burning sun.... I could speak for the slave; John Brown could fight for the slave. I could live for the slave; John Brown could die for the slave."

Chapter Ten

Enter Lincoln

THE FATEFUL PRESIDENTIAL contest of 1860 offered the American citizens an array of candidates; the Democratic party had been split into factions. Proslavery citizens favored stern-jawed Vice President John Breckinridge; northern moderates wanted Illinois Senator Stephen Douglas, the "Little Giant." Abraham "Honest Abe" Lincoln was the candidate of the Republicans, who were opposed to spreading slavery into new territories. The Constitutional Union party, set on preserving national unity at any cost, had John Bell of Tennessee as their candidate, and Gerrit Smith,

Jefferson Davis, "the Reluctant President," was leader of the Confederate States of America. He was a brilliant statesman and though his loyalties were with the South, he sought to prevent the war at the beginning.

Douglass's friend, was running on a strong antislavery platform.

Douglass began by campaigning for Smith, who had supported John Brown financially and had backed Douglass's newspaper. As the election drew close, Douglass realized, however, that Smith had no chance of winning and decided to back Lincoln "with firmer faith and more ardent hope than ever before."

The two Democratic candidates led in the popular vote, but the division in the party gave Lincoln the electoral vote. Lincoln's victory was, tragically, the signal to secession, first of South Carolina, which seceded from the Union on December 20, 1860. Many were angry with the abolitionists for having divided the nation, and in Boston Douglass was insulted, attacked, and thrown down a staircase.

In February of 1861, six more southern states—Georgia, Florida, Mississippi, Alabama, Louisiana, and Texas—seceded. A separate government under the name of the Confederate States of America was formed, with the dignified, austere Jefferson Davis of Mississippi as president.

President Lincoln's inaugural address in March disappointed Douglass, because Lincoln promised to uphold the Fugitive Slave Act and not interfere with slavery in the states where it was already established. In Lincoln's mind, his first priority was to restore the Union, not to end slavery.

As early as 1837, Lincoln had referred to the injustice and impracticality of slavery. The answer he saw then was to colonize the black man: to send him back to Africa or the West Indies. He had learned more by now; morally he was all for black rights but emotionally he still resisted. He was honest enough to admit his confusion.

Douglass began to despair, and even he thought of organizing a black emigration to the Caribbean nation of Haiti. Beginning in 1791, a rebellion led by Toussaint L'Ouverture, a self-educated former slave, had liberated all slaves and finally defeated both the British and the French. In 1802 Napoleon sent a force to subdue the Haitians. They offered stubborn resistance, even after Toussaint was taken by trickery, and the first black republic had been established in 1804. Perhaps this would be the place for American blacks, Douglass thought, ready to give up on the United States.

On April 12, 1861, Confederate troops bombarded Fort Sumter, a federal installation in the harbor of Charleston, South Carolina. Hostilities in the War between the States had officially begun. The fort surrendered a day later. Lincoln called for 75,000 troops to be mustered to put down the rebellion of seven southern states, whereupon Virginia, Tennessee, North Carolina, and Arkansas immediately joined the Confederacy. Four other slave states—Delaware, Maryland, Missouri, and Kentucky—remained in the Union.

The two sides prepared for battle, the North with its twenty-three states and population of twenty-two million against the South's eleven states and nine million people (including three and a half million slaves). The issues were complex, but basically the North was fighting to preserve the Union; the South for the right to secede and establish a nation that guaranteed a person's right to own slaves.

For Frederick Douglass and many others, the Civil War was a battle to end slavery forever. Douglass believed and stated frequently that the only choice for the nation was abolition or destruction. His two immediate goals were emancipation of all slaves in the Confederacy and the Union border states, and the right of blacks to enlist in the armies of the North. "I am for the war, for the Union, in any and every event."

Douglass traveled tirelessly, calling for Lincoln to grant slaves their freedom. "It is affirmed that the negro, if emancipated, could not take care of himself. My answer to this is, let him have a fair chance to try it. For two hundred years he has taken care of himself and his master into the bargain." But the president was slow to approve measures that would confiscate slaves in captured areas of the South; he was afraid that, if he passed laws that emancipated the slaves, the Union's border states might rebel and join the Confederacy, and he could ill afford to lose more states. However, on April 16, 1862, he signed a bill outlawing slavery in Washington, D.C.

As the war dragged on, costing more and more in lives and suffering, Lincoln did decide on stronger measures. In the summer of 1862, he drafted an order emancipating the slaves in the Confederate states. He was just waiting for the North to win a major battle before he issued the proclamation; it happened on the night of December 31, 1862, after the bloody battle of Antietam in Maryland. The Emancipation Proclamation declared that as of the next day all slaves in areas not held by Union troops were free. This appeased the by now impatient radical Republicans in Congress and was a big step forward to all abolitionists. Finally, the end of slavery was in

The death toll in the Civil War was the largest of any American war. The battle of Antietam, near Sharpsburg, Maryland, was the first on Union soil, and it was the bloodiest up to that time.

Considered a Union victory only because the heavy casualties forced Lee to retreat south again, it was after Antietam that Lincoln decided to issue his Emancipation Proclamation.

sight. Douglass and friends gathered at the telegraph office.... "We were watching...by the dim light of the stars for the dawn of a new day..., we were longing for the answer to the agonizing prayers of centuries." After the proclamation had been read, Douglass led in singing a hymn with the chorus, "This is the year of jubilee!" Their day of independence had dawned at last.

He wrote, "Unquestionably, for weal or for woe, the First of January is to be the most memorable day in American Annals. The Fourth of July was great, but the First of January, when we consider it in all its relations and bearings, is incompatibly greater. The one had respect to the mere political birth of a nation; the last concerns the national life and character and is to determine whether that life and character shall be radiantly glorious with all high and noble virtues, or infamously blackened, forevermore...."

In January 1863, Congress authorized black enlistment in the Union army. The Massachusetts 54th Regiment was the first black unit to be formed; one of the first to enlist was Charles Douglass, closely followed by his brother Lewis. The governor of the state asked Frederick Douglass to assist in recruitment. He wrote a passionate editorial, "Men of Color, to Arms," urging blacks to end in a day the bondage of centuries, earn their equality, and show their patriotism. "Action! Action! not criticism, is the plain duty of this hour.... Who would be free, themselves must strike the blow. Better even to die free than live slaves...."

The regiment's first attack was on Fort Wagner, and among the foremost who mounted the rampart was Sergeant-Major Lewis H. Douglass, shouting, "Come on, boys, and fight for God and Governor Andrew!" His sword was shot from his side, but both he and his brother survived the contest.

Earn their equality? Well, the black soldiers were paid half of what white soldiers received, were given inferior weapons as well as less training. Officers could not be chosen out of their ranks. Besides, captured black soldiers would be put into slavery or shot. When Douglass found out about the blatant inequality in the army, he stopped working for recruitment, published his complaints ("In peace and in war, I am content with nothing short of equal and exact justice"), and asked for an interview with the president. Lincoln granted the request in the summer of 1863.

The two men liked each other immediately. "I at once felt myself in the presence of an honest man, one whom I could love, honor , and trust without reserve or doubt," said Douglass. Lincoln took Douglass's complaints about the treatment of black soldiers seriously.

Douglass's account of his visit to the White House is worth special mention. "I tell you I felt big there. Let me tell you how I got to him; because everybody can't get to him.... The manner of getting to him gave me an idea that the cause was rolling on. The stair-way was crowded with applicants.... They were white; and as I was the only dark spot among them, I expected to have to wait at least half a day; I had heard of men waiting a week; but in two minutes after I sent in my card, the messenger came out and respectfully invited 'Mr. Douglass' in. I could hear, in the eager multitude outside as they saw me pressing and elbowing my way through, the remark, 'Yes, d—n it, I knew they would let the nigger through,' in a kind of despairing voice—a Peace Democrat, I suppose. When I went in, the President was sitting in his usual position, with his feet in different parts of the room, taking it easy."

Shortly afterwards the Secretary of War offered Douglass a commission on the staff of General Lorenzo Thomas. He waited at home for the commission, which never arrived. A black officer? No, the army was not ready for that.

His son Frederick, Jr., had now also joined the Union army. More than 200,000 blacks enlisted, and 38,000 were killed or wounded in Civil War battles. The black soldiers comprised about ten percent of the troops of the North, and they distinguished themselves in many engagements.

By mid-1864 the war was slowly turning in favor of the North.

Douglass was concerned about the fate of blacks after the war. Lincoln did not seem overly interested in voting rights for blacks. Discrimination continued.

In May 1864, with the presidential elections approaching, however, Douglass and others, who had thought of supporting John C. Fremont, realized that, with the popular general George McClellan (who was for peace with the South, leaving slaves in bondage) running, they better throw their support behind Lincoln, and Douglass did his utmost to secure Lincoln's reelection.

Douglass and Lincoln had a second meeting in August 1864. Lincoln asked Douglass to draw up plans for leading slaves out of the South. Douglass was convinced that Lincoln himself cared about blacks but also that the

Abraham Lincoln, seen here with his cabinet, issued the Emancipation Proclamation, declaring all slaves within the states in rebellion against the Union to be free as of January 1, 1863. From a tactical standpoint, he hoped that this would give the

North a moral advantage and prevent France and England from entering the war on the side of the South. It worked; the European nations remained neutral, leaving the Confederacy to fight on its own against overwhelming odds.

president stood rather alone and that his views were unpopular even among many in the North, weary of a war setting brother against brother.

The North won a series of victories, and Lincoln was easily reelected in November. By the end of the year, the suffering South was retreating. Sixteen days after the new state constitution abolishing slavery had been confirmed, Douglass went to Maryland and parts of Virginia, even lecturing in Baltimore, where he had once lived as a slave. He saw his sister Eliza after twenty-eight years; although she had no schooling, she had worked hard and had bought freedom for herself and her nine children. He tried to see Sophia Auld as well, now a widow since Hugh Auld had died, but was coldly rebuffed and ordered from her home.

Back again, Douglass attended Lincoln's second inaugural address in the nation's capital. As he was sitting in the Senate gallery, a white man came up behind him, put a hand on his shoulder, and asked roughly for his name. His first impulse was to reply angrily, but after a glance at the questioner, he said, "as gently as any sucking dove," "Fred Douglass, sir." "What! The original Fred Douglass?" "The original Fred Douglass, sir."

"Oh," said the man and went out while people around chuckled.

But government officials refused to allow him or any other black to attend the evening reception in the White House. None of his skin color had ever done so. When the president heard about this, Douglass was ushered inside, where the president greeted him with the words, "Here comes my friend Douglass," and proceeded to ask his opinion of the inaugural address. Douglass pronounced it "a sacred effort."

No directives had been given to keep any blacks out; the officers had simply followed old usage. "In my experience," Douglass said, "the way to break down an unreasonable custom is to contradict it in practice."

In April General Robert E. Lee surrendered to the Union commander Ulysses S. Grant at Appomattox Court House in Virginia. On April 9, 1865, the Civil War was finally over.

But President Lincoln was assassinated by a proslavery fanatic, John Wilkes Booth, while attending a play at Ford's Theater in Washington on April 14 (Good Friday). He died the following morning.

In the middle of his and the nation's sorrow, Douglass rejoiced: the war to end slavery had been won.

Chapter Eleven

No More Slavery, but...

THE THIRTEENTH Amendment to the United States Constitution was ratified in December 1865, officially abolishing slavery in all the United States: "Neither slavery nor involuntary servitude, except as a punishment for crime whereof the party shall have been duly convicted, shall exist within the United States, or any place subject to their jurisdiction."

Now followed the Reconstruction era in the South, during which the eleven Confederate states were slowly incorporated into the Union. The war had been costly in many ways,

---

Political parties took strong stances on slavery. The candidate of the newly formed Republican party, "Honest" Abraham Lincoln, known for his opposition to slavery, won the election of 1860.

and in some cases had nourished rather than canceled the hatred and intolerance.

And Frederick Douglass? About forty-seven years old and having won the fight to which he had dedicated his life, he entertained some thoughts about settling down on a farm, leading the quiet life.

Soon, however, he found out that everything was not coming up roses for those of a less than rosy complexion. White America was still painfully ambivalent. Douglass was discovering that the freedom was of the abstract variety, often expressed in luminous rhetoric. Although the Union army remained in the South to offer protection to ex-slaves, they could only do so much. Furthermore, Lincoln's successor, Andrew Johnson from Tennessee, was not overly keen on helping southern blacks. In the months immediately after the war, the whites were in power still, and they could and would keep blacks in abject poverty and in servants' positions. If an ex-slave had no permanent employment, he or she could be arrested and fined heavily. Since they would not have money for the fines, they would be hired out to local industries—they were still virtual slaves. When they found work, they were paid less than white workers, they were prevented from buying land, and so on.

Thaddeus Stevens urged that the government give each of the black former slaves forty acres and a mule, but Congress never saw fit to fulfill this promise.

Garrison suggested that the abolitionist movement disband, but Douglass countered with his statement that slavery would not be gone until "the black man has the ballot." Two senators, strongly against slavery—Thaddeus Stevens and Charles Sumner—joined the fight for voting rights for blacks.

Douglass kept on speaking publicly, pointing out that the former slave owners were regaining control of the South, for all practical purposes. In February of 1866 he spoke with Andrew Johnson, the president, in a meeting to which he brought his son Lewis and three other black leaders. The president told them frankly that he would continue to support the white people in the South and was not going to go out on a limb for the black voting rights. Johnson compared himself to Moses and complained of so great a hostility between poor whites and blacks as to make it impossible to let "both be thrown together at the ballot-box." Douglass quoted Cicero, who had said in the first century, "Freedom is participation in power." The talkative president, unwilling to listen (to the point that Douglass felt

The Confederacy held out as long as it could, with its forces west of the Mississippi not surrendering until well after Jefferson Davis had been captured by the Union army. In the months

after the war, white southerners attempted to remain in office and slaveholders tried to keep their newly freed "property," until the Union army took full control throughout the South.

obliged to make his reply in print), also recommended that colored people leave the country. America, the mother of exiles, was showing little motherly concern for her black children. "Sometimes I feel like a motherless child," singers sang with conviction.

As Douglass and others kept on arguing their case, he declaring it a wonder that negroes (note that the word was not capitalized until the beginning of this century) were still alive, public opinion was slowly swaying to their side. Even members of Congress felt that the ex-slaves, now called "freedmen," should be given more than freedom without opportunities. They listened to Douglass's words, "Emancipation granted the Negro freedom to hunger, freedom to winter amid the rains of heaven. Emancipation was freedom and famine at the same time."

Douglass attended a meeting in Philadelphia where the radical Republicans were calling for black suffrage. He spoke in his impassioned way—although silently noting that many Republicans were far from ready to associate with any black man on an equal footing.

Douglass was not indifferent to the sight of injustice anywhere. The outrageous way in which the Chinese were treated made him speak up on their behalf. He did the same for Native Americans, Mexicans, and Indians (from India), finding racism a product of ignorance and a host of other factors, encompassing selfishness, arrogance, aggression, and greed. What is racism? The dogma that one ethnic group is condemned by nature to hereditary inferiority? What is the logical conclusion? Genocide?

He went to the National Loyalist's Convention in Philadelphia in 1866 as an appointed delegate from Rochester. (Most of the other delegates were white.) Walking in the convention parade, the only person of color to do so, he spotted Amanda Auld Sears among the bystanders. It was her mother, Lucretia Auld, who had given him his first pair of pants and sent him to Baltimore. Now the daughter of Lucretia and the stepchild of mean Rowena had traveled to Philadelphia with her two children to see and hear the famous Frederick Douglass. The next day, he went to see her; they remained in touch from then on, and in 1877, when she was dying, she called him to her bedside. Later, when the Sears family had financial trouble, they turned to Frederick Douglass for help.

In July 1867, President Johnson asked Douglass to head the Freedmen's Bureau to oversee government programs, including reading classes, for southern blacks. Douglass was tempted—this was the first time a black man had been offered a major government post—but he realized also that by accepting, he would make it seem as if Johnson was a friend of blacks. In the end, he refused to serve under a man whose policies he detested.

The year 1867 was also when he was reunited with his older brother Perry after forty years of separation. He embraced his "dear old slavery-scarred and long lost brother" and built a cottage next to his house, where Perry and his family of six were installed.

In 1868, Douglass campaigned for the Republican candidate, Ulysses S. Grant (former commander in chief of the Union army), whose slogan was "Let us have peace."

In a famous speech, "The Work Before Us," Douglass attacked the Democratic party for ignoring black citizens and warned about the rise in the South of white supremacist organizations such as the Ku Klux Klan, which attempted to scare blacks out of their legal rights. "Rebellion has been subdued, slavery abolished, and peace proclaimed, and yet our work is not yet done," he said.

Grant won the presidency with ease, and the Fifteenth Amendment passed through

Ulysses S. Grant, who had led the North to victory, ran for the presidency in 1868, and Frederick Douglass actively campaigned for his election. However, in 1872, Douglass briefly considered opposing Grant by supporting the Equal Rights party.

Congress (the one granting the right to vote to all male citizens, regardless of their race). It was sent for ratification to the states. This caused a temporary rift between Douglass and the women suffragists, since women were not included in the voting rights. He tried to explain that the voting rights for blacks had to be pushed through without delay, while women's rights, although also important, lacked the same urgency. "When women because they are women are dragged from their homes and hung upon lamp-posts," he said, then there would be real urgency. (Women did not receive the right to vote until 1920.)

On March 30, 1870, President Grant declared that the amendment had been ratified and adopted. By this time, Douglass could look back at quite a long list of achievements. Blacks were elected to state legislatures and even won seats in Congress. Hiram Revels of Mississippi became the first black senator and Joseph Rainey of South Carolina the first black in the House of Representatives.

The 1870s offered Douglass many honors. He was asked to become the editor for the Washington, D.C., newspaper, the *New National Era*. He did not just accept the post, he bought the paper and ran it until it folded in 1874, thereby having a forum for his ideas for a few years—while losing money, unfortunately.

In 1872 the family home of Douglass was destroyed by a suspicious fire, and he decided to move his family to Washington, D.C., the center of political activity. Even though he was asked to run as vice-president for the Equal Rights party, he decided instead to campaign hard for the reelection of President Grant, who did win. Douglass was then chosen as one of the two electors-at-large from New York (the men who carried the sealed envelope with the result of the state voting to the capital). He expected that, after this honor, he would be given a position in the Grant administration. When no such post was forthcoming, Douglass returned to the lecture circuit.

In 1874, when his newspaper folded, he accepted the position as president of the troubled Freedmen's Savings and Trust Company, founded to encourage blacks to invest and save their money. The bank collapsed, however, even though Douglass put most of his own money into it and appealed to the Congress for help. Many black depositors lost their money, which hurt Douglass more than his own losses.

He kept on lecturing, now including other

subjects besides black rights: women's suffrage, John Brown, and...Scandinavian folklore.

During his travels he encountered racial prejudice on a regular basis, and each time he would protest by sending letters to the local newspapers. His name attached to these protests gave them added weight.

In 1875, he was cheered by the passage of the Civil Rights Act, for which he had campaigned, giving blacks the right to equal treatment in theaters, inns, and other public places.

In 1877, Rutherford B. Hayes was inaugurated as president of the United States, and Douglass finally received his political post, United States Marshal for the District of Columbia. He was criticized by some blacks for accepting, since the government had just agreed to remove most federal troops from the South, where "a murderous warfare is going on against the newly emancipated citizens." He spoke out against this abandonment of southern blacks but still accepted the post as another honor to a member of his people and therefore of importance in the general state of things. "An innovation upon long established usage," is what he said.

Also, he was close to sixty years old, and the constant traveling was taking its toll. As marshal for Washington, he had a large staff, and he had purchased a home on fifteen acres, where cedars, oaks, and hickories grew. He christened the twenty-room house "Cedar Hill," a slight smile on his lips because the original owner had stipulated that the plot should never be owned by a Negro or an Irishman! His children and grandchildren were always welcome for extended visits.

In 1877, he also made a trip back to the plantation where he had worked as a slave and even visited his old master, Thomas Auld, who greeted his ex-property as "Marshal Douglas." The two men spoke for a long time and parted on rather good terms.

After the 1880 election of James Garfield as president, Douglass was appointed to the post of Recorder of Deeds for Washington, D.C. He stayed on this post for five years, since it gave him ample time for writing and speaking about and for justice. The job was not yet done. As he said, "Slavery, ignorance, stupidity, servility, poverty, dependence, are undesirable conditions. When these cease to be coupled with color, there will be no color-line drawn." In 1881 he published the third of his autobiographical volumes, *Life and Times of Frederick Douglass*.

Chapter Twelve

Minister to Haiti

ON AUGUST 4, 1882, Anna Douglass, who had suffered from rheumatism for many years, died after a four-week bout with debilitating paralysis. "The main pillar of my life has fallen," said her husband of forty-four years. He observed the traditional year of mourning, but the vital man was not ready for the lonely life. On January 24, 1884, he married Helen Pitts, a white woman of forty-six, nearly twenty years younger than he was. Helen was born in Rochester, of colonial and revolutionary ancestry (entitled to membership in the Daughters of the American

With the surrender of General Robert E. Lee at Appomattox Court House, Virginia, in April of 1865, the Civil War was virtually over. In the weeks that followed, southern slaves were freed, but their rights were yet to be defined.

Revolution, had she so desired). She had been graduated in 1859 from Mt. Holyoke Female Seminary. Late in the 1870s, she had met Douglass through her uncle, who owned the estate adjacent to Cedar Hill. She had been working in the recorder's office as Douglass's secretary. She was described as a woman "of dignity and respectability," a tall, gracious person, totally devoted to her husband.

The marriage caused heavy criticism from whites and blacks alike. Whites mumbled about a ban on interracial marriage—blacks felt that he had showed contempt for his own. Some thought she had married him for his money. His housekeeper of ten years left, his children never quite accepted his new wife, and her father never forgave his daughter for marrying a black man. Her mother and sister, on the other hand, quickly became reconciled to the marriage and spent much time at Cedar Hill.

Douglass saw no inconsistency between his beliefs, his loyalties, and his marriage to a woman he loved. (He himself was the fruit of a black slave mother and a white man.) He had never worked for a world in which black and white were separated. He believed truly in justice and freedom for all, a raceless world in which color was simply a matter of description, if mentioned at all. He spoke of an "instinctive consciousness of the common brotherhood of man," seeing that as human beings we all belong to one species. We might appreciate cultural differences, respect political and religious differences, but we do well to ignore race. He was tiring of the constant referral to someone as "black" or "white" or whatever.

He did keep a scrapbook containing the letters of outrage about his marriage; the most irate comment came from a Virginia newspaper, calling him "a lecherous old African Solomon."

He took the criticism from his black compatriots more seriously but felt he was misunderstood by them, and his marital bliss overshadowed all adverse reactions, for he could not help but enjoy being married to an intellectual equal. Comments from friends reveal that the two were truly in love and that "happiness radiated from them both."

In 1884, Grover Cleveland, a Democrat, was elected president. Douglass resigned his post as recorder of deeds and traveled with his young wife to England. He visited his old friend Julia Griffith as well as the two women who had bought him his freedom four decades earlier. He and Helen went on to France,

After the Emancipation Proclamation, Congress authorized black troops for the Civil War. Frederick Douglass helped recruit volunteers for the first regiment, the 54th Regiment of

Massachusetts Volunteer Infantry, seen here as portrayed in the motion picture Glory. *Two of Douglass's sons, Charles and Lewis, joined the famed 54th Volunteers.*

spending two months in Paris, which he called "a city of taste and terrors, of heroes and horrors, of beauty, barricades, and bottles." They continued to Italy, and he found Rome "neither pleasant to the eye nor to the thought," especially not "the vacant, bare-legged, grimy monks, who have taken a vow neither to work nor to wash." He did enjoy the ruins of the past, however, and Paganini's violin in Genoa fascinated him, a music lover and violinist himself, as did the unveiling of a statue of Galileo. From there they went to Egypt, where the "silent, solemn, measureless desert" made an impression, and to Greece. He found Athens fascinating, filled with memories from another era, and with a people who loved freedom dearly.

Returning to Washington in time for the seventy-ninth anniversary of the birth of Abraham Lincoln on February 12, 1888, he spoke of Lincoln as the man who "went up before his Maker with four millions of broken fetters in his arms."

Later that year, Douglass went on a tour to the Deep South. Seeing the ramshackle shacks in which poor black tenant farmers lived, he realized that he was out of touch with his people and their needs, and that many had made little progress from the barbarism of slavery, being in a deplorable condition since their emancipation, which had been "keeping the word of promise to the ear and breaking it to the heart."

He pointed out that, in many cases, the highest wages paid a man were "eight dollars a month, and this he receives only in orders on a store, which, in many cases, is owned by his employer." Thus, "he struggles from year to year, but like a man in a morass, the more he struggles, the deeper he sinks."

Returning to Washington for the twenty-sixth anniversary of the Emancipation Proclamation, Douglass spoke with rage about the exploitation of blacks and the denial of their civil rights. Again, the black laborers looked to him as their leader, some of them having felt for a period of time that he had become too involved with the rich and famous to have bonds with them.

In 1888 Benjamin Harrison, a corporation lawyer from Indiana and a Republican, replaced Cleveland in office and offered Douglass the appointment as the American consul-general to Haiti. Harrison's selection of a black man brought criticism from those who felt that the need to obtain commercial concessions demanded a white minister. Douglass dismissed the criticism with the assertion that

The 54th Massachusetts Volunteer Infantry follows its white officers into battle against Confederate forces in this scene from

the Edward Zwick film, Glory, *a Tri-Star production. Both free and newly freed blacks fought in the last year of the war.*

there was always a demand made for a white man when there was five thousand dollars attached to the offer. He accepted the appointment, always having been interested in Haiti, and arrived there on October 8, 1889, after eleven stormy days at sea.

Douglass loved everything about Haiti, except the climate. The Haitians were proud to have the famous champion of black rights among them (and told him he looked like Victor Hugo). He treated the small republic and its people with utmost respect. Unfortunately he became involved in the United States government's attempts to establish a naval base on the northwest tip of Haiti and the attempt to win concessions for American business. Douglass opposed this, knowing how much the Haitians feared American domination and with it the loss of their sovereignty. The Americans blamed Douglass when Haiti turned down the naval base.

In 1891, his health being less than robust and the tropical climate being hard on both him and his wife, he resigned and returned to the United States, where he resumed a quiet life at Cedar Hill. He spent much time writing and relaxing by playing the violin, with Helen accompanying him on the piano. He continued with his speaking assignments, and in 1893 the Haitian government asked him to be its representative to the World's Columbian Exposition, the international fair held in Chicago. He was the only black American to perform a major role at the exposition.

In his continued writing, he emphasized the need for blacks to avail themselves of the opportunities for education. His attitudes shaped many of those who came after him: Booker T. Washington, Ida Wells-Barnett, W.E.B. Du Bois, and numerous others.

He also advocated the gospel of wealth, saying that his people "would never be respected until they respected themselves, and that they would never respect themselves until they had the means to live respectably." It was not that Douglass worshipped the almighty dollar, rather that he believed that "the destruction of the poor is their poverty." For a balanced life, he advised the youth to seek the things of the mind and the spirit but added, "Aristotle and Pericles are all right; get all that, too; but get money besides, and plenty of it." He also said, "What we call money is only stored labor."

In his final years he devoted much time to speaking out against the country's lack of concern about the lynchings of blacks in the

United States. He wrote an essay, "The Lesson of the Hour; Why the Negro is Lynched," blaming the wealthy southern elite for much since they forever encouraged what would "keep the Negroes in their place." He understood that violence was an integral aspect of the racist repression, recalling the first vicious whipping he saw, that of his young Aunt Hester. "It was the blood-stained gate, the entrance to the hell of slavery…." The lynchings during the last years of his life likewise struck him "with awful force." (Note: Between 1884 and 1900, there were twenty-five hundred lynchings, mostly of black men, in the United States. Humanitarians everywhere assailed this lawless, horrible trend.)

He wanted to see America as a home for people of all colors and continued to speak out against colonizing blacks in Africa or other lands. "We are here and are here to stay," he said.

On February 20, 1895, he attended a meeting of women's rights activists in Washington. Escorted to the speakers' platform by his old friend Susan B. Anthony, he was warmly greeted by the activist leaders and a cheering crowd, giving him a standing ovation. That night, as he told his wife about his day during dinner and before leaving for a speaking

The late actor Raymond St. Jacques, known for his varied and sometimes controversial roles, portrayed Frederick Douglass in the Edward Zwick film, Glory, *a Tri-Star production.*

engagement at seven, he fell to his knees. At first she thought he was, as usual, dramatizing his story, but he was sinking lower and lower, losing consciousness. He had been struck by a massive heart attack—and died, quickly and peacefully. It might be assumed that he was in his seventy-seventh year. Or it could have been his seventy-eighth year, since he never knew his exact birthday, although he had taken to celebrating it for years on February 14.

Crowds gathered at the Washington church where he lay in state. Black public schools closed for the day. His people came to honor him. So did politicians, educators, women's rights activists, and many, many more. There existed hardly an American whose life had not been touched by Frederick Douglass, ex-slave and great hero.

Helen Douglass and his three surviving children—Rosetta, Lewis, and Charles—took his body to Rochester, where he lay in state at the City Hall with throngs of people filing by. He was buried at Mt. Hope. But the hope and the belief in the sanctity of life, liberty, and happiness he had nourished, made realistic, and seen partially fulfilled were not buried. The same hope lives with and inside us: the hope for a world where freedom truly reigns.

Chronology

1817–18	Born as the slave Frederick Augustus Washington Bailey on a Maryland plantation.
1826	Travels to Baltimore to work for Hugh and Sophia Auld.
1833	Returns to plantation to work for Thomas Auld.
1934	Is hired out as farmhand to Edward Covey.
1835	Is hired out as farmhand to William Freeland.
1836	Escape plan fails. Is imprisoned, then sent back to Hugh Auld in Baltimore. Learns a trade (caulking).
1837	Meets Anna Murray.
1838	Escapes to New York. Marries Anna Murray. Changes his name to Frederick Douglass.
1839	Daughter Rosetta is born.
1840	Son Lewis Henry is born.
1841	Speaks at Anti-Slavery Convention; is asked to go on tour as a speaker.
1842	Son Frederick is born.
1844	Son Charles is born.
1845	*Narrative of the Life of Frederick Douglass, An American Slave* is published; travels to England on lecture tour.
1846	British friends buy him from Hugh Auld; Frederick Douglass is a free man in the eyes of the law.
1847	Returns to the United States; begins publishing *North Star*.
1848	Attends women's rights convention.
1849	Daughter Annie is born.
1859	Meets with John Brown for the last time; flees to Canada when Brown is executed. Begins

	lecture tour in England.
1860	Daughter Annie dies. Returns to the United States.
1863	Meets with President Abraham Lincoln for the first time.
1864	Meets again with President Lincoln; attends inaugural address and reception.
1866	Meets with President Andrew Johnson.
1867	Declines President Johnson's offer to head Freedmen's Bureau.
1868	Campaigns for Ulysses S. Grant.
1870	Becomes editor and owner of the *New National Era*.
1872	Family home is destroyed by a suspicious fire; the family moves to Washington.
1874	Becomes president of the troubled Freedmen's Savings and Trust Company.
1877	Becomes U.S. Marshal; makes a return trip to the plantation.
1880	Appointed recorder of deeds for Washington, D.C.
1881	*Life and Times of Frederick Douglass* is published.
1882	Anna Douglass dies.
1884	Douglass marries Helen Pitts.
1888	Becomes American consul-general to Haiti.
1891	Resigns post and returns home.
1895	Dies in Washington, D.C.

Index

Picture Credits

The Marine Research Center: pp. 8, 36, 38-39, 44, 47, 50-51, 55, 69, 83, 98-99, 128-129; Players International Archives: pp. 73, 78-79; The Bettman Archives: pp. 11, 16-17, 24, 31, 33, 60, 64-65, 85-86, 93, 102, 138, 154, 168; African-American West Coast Archives: pp. 20-21, 27; U.S. National Parks: pp. 107, 112-114, 120-121, 124, 144-145, 150-151, 158-159, 163; Eddie Brandt's Saturday Matinee: pp. 172-173, 176-177; Contemporary-Korman Artists, Ltd.: p. 181.

Additional Reading

Douglass, Frederick. *Narrative of the Life of Frederick Douglass, An American Slave*; Anchor Books, Doubleday, 1845, 1963.

Foner, Philip S. *The Life and Writings of Frederick Douglass: Early Years 1817–1849*; International Publishers, New York, 1950.

Huggins, Nathan Irvin. *Slave and Citizen: The Life of Frederick Douglass*; Little, Brown, Boston, 1980.

Quarles, Benjamin. *Frederick Douglass*; The Associated Publishers, Inc., 1948.

MARIANNE RUUTH lives in Los Angeles, California, where she reports, with emphasis on the cinema, for newspapers and magazines in France, Portugal, Sweden, and other European countries. She is a former president of the Hollywood Foreign Press Association and the author of numerous books, including *Stevie Wonder*; *Eddie Murphy*; *The Supremes: Triumph and Tragedy*; *Cruel City: The Dark Side of Hollywood's Rich and Famous*. For the Melrose Square Black American Series, she is the author of biographies of *Bill Cosby*, *Nat King Cole*, *Sarah Vaughan*, and *Oprah Winfrey*. A contributing writer and researcher for *The Chronicle of the Twentieth Century* and *The Chronicle of America*, she has chaired Women in Film International and is a member of Mensa.